Nātya Sāstra Series No. 7

A Glossary of Nātya Sāstra

Compiled by
Naresh Gupta

Second Revised Edition

Sri Satguru Publications
A Division of
Indian Books Centre
Delhi-India

Sri Satgur Publications
A Division of
Indian Books Centre
24/4, Shakti Nagar,
Delhi-110007
INDIA

First Edition : Delhi, 1994,
Second Revised Edition : Delhi, 2021

ISBN : 81-7030-394-X.
: 978-81-7030-3947

Printed at Infinity Imaging Systems, Delhi - 110053

Abhilasi Movement : An expectant glance.

Abhitapta Movement : The pupils look dull due to the movements of the eyelids. The glance is full of distress and pain.

Abhunga : The chest is drawn inward. The back is raised and the shoulder is slightly bent forward and slackened.

Acchurita : The dancer performs Nupura carana, revolves the back, and moves the hands in Vyarhsita. The back is revolved again. Alataka follows on the left side of the body, Suci is done at the same place, and Ailgahara is concluded by performing the Karihasta and Kattchinna Karanas. The eight Karanas in the Acchurita Ailgahara are Nupura, Bhramara, Vyarhsita, Alataka, Nitamba, Suci, Karihasta and Katicchinna.

Adalu : The dancer jumps in Sulu with her feet waving like the wings of a bird and turns round.

Adbhuta Movement : The eyelids are curled, the eyes are charmingly opened and raised in wonder.

Addaskhalitika : The dancer stamps one foot obliquely.

Addita : One foot in Agratalasancara rubs its forepart or the back against the other. The right foot moves in Udghattita, then turns round and performs Askandita and strikes the ground. The left foot performs Sakatasya. The right foot performs Prsthapasarpi and Casagati while the left foot performs Addita. Again the right foot performs Apasarpita and the left foot performs Bhramaraka.

Adhahksipta : To bend the toes repeatedly.

Adhama Movement : The pupils are slightly visible in winking eyes which are turned down. The eyes may either wink very often or be steady.

Adhogata : The head is bent down.

Adhomukha : The arms point to the ground.

Adhuta : The head is obliquely raised upwards once.

Adhyardha : The right foot performs Janita and Aspandita successively while the left foot performs Apasarpi. Again the right foot performs Sakasasya. The dancer moves round.

Adhyardhika : The left foot rests on the heel of the right foot and then it is drawn away.

Adrstaprsthatulla : The dancer performs the Karihasta Gati and others at intervals according to her wish. It is performed to Raccatala, nor too fast nor too slowly and has proper yatis. The hands are moved in various beautiful ways.

Adrutalanrtya : The dancer dances in a slow tempo to Adrutala. Udgraha and Dhruvaka are sung.

Agraga Movements of Shanks : The dancer steps forward quickly.

Agratalasaincara Movements of Shanks : The dancer raises her heels, putting her big toes forward and contracting the rest of her toes.

Ahvana : To invite.

Akampita : The head is moved slowly up and down.

Akasabhramari : The dancer jumps with her feet stretched and kept wide apart. Then she revolves her body.

Akekara Movement : The eyelids are slightly contracted at then corners. They are joined together. and they are half closed while the pupils are repeatedly raised.

Aksipta : The hands are moved in Aksiptarecita. The dancer looks downward with one side bent. The Kuncita foot is thrown up and then placed on the Aksipta foot. The shanks are crossed in Svastika.

Aksiptarecita : The dancer performs Svastikapada in Recita and does the same with the hands. He separates them, and lifts them with the same (Recita) movement, and performs Udvrtta, Aksipta and Uromandala. The Ailgahara ends with the Nitamba, Karihasta and Katicchinna Karanas.

Akuntcita : The wrist is bent inward.

Alaga : The dancer jumps up with her face downwards and comes down to the front. Then she stands still performing Kukkusasana.

Alagabhramari : The dancer stands in the Vaisnava Sthana. Then she stands on the left foot and rotates her body obliquely.

Alagancita : The dancer performs Alaga first and quickly moves doing Ancita.

Alapadma : The Alpallava hands are raised to the shoulders.

Alapadmavartana : The Alapadma hands are moved in Vyavrtta.

Alapallava : The Alapallava hands are moved from the chest to the shoulder in Udvestita Karala.

Alasa Movement : The eyes move away from the desired objects.

Alata : One foot is extended backwards. Then it is moved and put inwards. Finally, it is thrown down on its heel. The dancer places one of her feet backwards and crosses it quickly with the other. The right foot performs Suci and the left foot performs Apakranta. The right foot again performs Parsvakranta while the left foot performs Alata.

Alatacakra : One hand moves towards the body and away.

Alataka : The dancer moves the hands in Vyarhsita, following this with Alataka, Urdhvajanu, Nikuncita, Ardhasuci, Viksipta, Udvrtta, Aksipta, Karihasta and Kasicchinna successively. One foot moves in Alata the right hand moves down from the shoulder. The right hand assumes Nitamba first and then Caturasra. The left side of the body performs Urdhvajanu with the left foot.

Alidha : The dancer performs Nupura with the left foot and with the other (right) foot performs Alataka and Aksipta. The dancer moves the hands in Vyarhsita, touching the top of the shoulders with the hands. Nupura should be performed with the left foot and Alataka with the right. Aksiptaka is performed with the same side of the body. The dancer places her left foot twenty-seven inches apart from the right foot. Her left hand is in Sikhara while her right hand is in Katakamukha. The Mandala Sthana is performed with the right foot extended by five talas from the other foot.

Alingana : Sarhyutahasta. The Pataka hands are crossed.

Alktrima : A natural look.

Alokita : To look quickly with widely opened eyes.

Amsancita : The hands are bent over the shoulders and they are moved in Vyavarta and Parivarta. The feet moves in Nikuna.

Amsaparyayanirgata : The hands form a Svastika while doing Kalasa and then they are stretched out alternatiely from the shoulders to the hips.

Amsavartanaka : The arms are raised and moved in Vartana near the wrists, shoulders, elbows and the fore-arms. The head is a little bent and the hands, with the palms turned down are moved on the ground in front. They are moved simultaneously or one after the other at the sides, to the left and the right.

Anandi Movement : The eyelids join in pleasure.

Anangangamotana : The hands are moved round near the shoulders.

Anangoddipana : The hands are kept on the chest. Then they are moved round one by one and brought near the shoulders.

Ancita : Hands are arched over the tips of the nose touching it. The arms move out from the chest and come back. The dancer stands in Sarna and then jumps straight up.

Ancita Movement : The pupils alternately move and stop.

Ancita Movements of Shanks : The dancer touches the ground with her heels and the foreparts of her feet while her toes are contracted.

Andolita Movement : Slow and oblique movement of the hips.

Andtara : The feet are joined at the front.

Angabhramari : The dancer stands and revolves her body with her feet kept one vitasti apart (Vitasti = Twelve angulas or nine inches).

Anghritadita : The dancer stretches her feet, jumps up and claps them.

Angulisamslista : Meeting the toes. Touching the big toe.

Anjali : The Pataka hands are put together.

Anjana : Nrtta-hasta. The Lalita hands are placed on the chest. Then they assume Kapota near the ear. Finally, Sandarilsa is done.

Antaralaga : The dancer raises her chest and touches her hips at the back with her head. The dancer jumps while arching her back and keeping her head between her shanks.

Antara Padmasana : The dancer jumps and extends her feet. Then she joins their soles in Padmasana.

Antargata : Turned inward.

Anulomaviloma : Trikonacri is done in the regular way and then in reverse. Then the feet are placed in the original position and Nikuttana is done.

Anulvana : An agitated look.

Anupaskrti : The eyes show affection through the corners.

Anutseka : The eyelids and the corners of the eyes are cast down.

Anuvrtta : To observe carefuly and quickly up and down.

Apakranta : The thighs are moved in Valana, one foot is raised and thrown sideways in Kuncita. The thighs are moved in Valita. The Apakranta Cari is performed, and the hands are moved in harmony.

Apaksepa : The dancer touches one of her thighs with the outer side of the other foot which is then moved near the hips.

Apakuncita : The dancer gradually moves backward with her feet bent.

Aparajita : The nine Karanas that are used in the Aparajita Angahara are Dandapada, Vyarhsita, Prasarpita, Nikuna, Ardhanikutta, Aksipta, Uromandala, Karihasta and Katicchinna. The Uromandala Karanas placing the hand in Viksipta and Aksipta followed by the Vyarhsita Karal The left hand and the left foot are moved at the same time. Two Nikuttakas are performed.

Apasarpita : The dancer moves only the hands in Vyarhsita, and then proceeds to Karihasta, Ardhasuci, Viksipta, Katicchinna, Drudvrtta, Aksipta, Karihasta and Katicchinna.

Apasrta Movement : To move out from the Vivartita position of the sides.

Apasyandita : It is Syandita done with the other foot.

Apaviddha : The hands are rotated near the throat and the navel at the left and right sides of the dancer. The right hand describes a circle and is placed on the thigh in Sukatunda. The left hand is placed on the chest in Khatakamukha. The hands are to be changed to Uro Mandala.

Aralakhataka Mukha : The Alapallava hands with their palms turned upwards should be changed to Padmakosa. This is also known as Aralakhataka or the hands in Arala are separated at the wrists.

Aralavartana : The hands are moved in Avestita and Udvestita.

Aratrika : The head is moved in a circular way touching the shoulders.

Ardhakuncita Movement of Knee : The hips are lowered.

Ardhamandalavartana : The hands are stretched and moved round, each from its own side of the chest and after moving in Avestana assume Arala.

Ardhamandalika : The dancer moves her feet outward dragging them against the ground one by one slowly in a circular way.

Ardhamattalli : The feet are drawn away from Skhalita and the left hand moves in Recita. The right hand is placed on the hips. Nitamba and Kesabandha vartanas are performed with the right hand. The feet are moved in agitation. The left hand assumes partial Recita.

Ardhamukula Movement : The eyes are half open and the pupils move slightly.

Ardhanikutta : The hands, facing each other, are bent between the head and the arms. Thus Ardhanikutta is the result of doing half of Nikutta. The dancer performs Nupurapada, rapidly moving the hands and the feet in harmony and revolving the back.

Ardharecita : The hands move away in Suc!mukha. The feet move in Nikutta. One side reposes in Saimata. The left hand is Caturasra and the right is Recita. The hands are moved in Recita and Udvartita.

Ardhasuci : The Alapadma hand is placed on the head and the right foot is in Suci. The left hand curved and bent.

Ardhasvastika : The feet cross each other in Svastika. The right hand is in Karihasta and the left hand is on the chest. The hands are placed on the hips in Paksapradyotaka and Ardhacandra.

Argala : One foot is stretched backward and the feet are kept apart by two talas and a half. The hands are moved in the same manner. The right foot is placed on the little toe of the left foot. The knees are kept apart by two talas and a half and they are motionless. The left hand in Alapallava is still and the right hand is a little stretched to the front.

Arocaka : The eyes are contracted at the corners.

Arta : A vacant look.

Asambhranta : A glance that notices the subtlest things.

Aspandita : The right foot performs Bhramara and the left foot performs Addita. The hips are turned round and the right foot performs Sakatasya and Drdudvrtta while the left foot makes Apasarpita. The right foot moves in Spandita and the left foot moves in Sakatasya and then strikes the ground violently.

Astabandhavihara : The hands are moved round first to the left and the right, then to the front and towards the back and then to the eight quarters, on all sides of the body.

Asvakranta : One foot is in Sarna while the toes of the other foot are curved. Then one foot in Suci may be either placed on the heel of the other which is in Sarna or kept apart.

Asvotplavana : The dancer jumps with both feet and places them together. Her hands are in Tripataka.

Aticakrabhramari : The dancer moves round placing her right hand on her hips.

Aticitra Movements of Shanks : The dancer revolves in the centre of the stage bending her toes.

Atikranta : One foot is placed forward after performing the Atikranta Cari. The hands are moved in harmony. The dancer raises one foot in Kuncita. She extends it forward and places it on the ground. The right foot performs Janita. The left foot performs Alata and then the right foot performs Parsvakranta. The left foot performs Suci while the right foot again performs Parsvakranta.

Avadhuta : The head is bent down once.

Avahithavartana : The hands move in Avahitha.

Avahittha : The left foot is in Sarna while the other is placed obliquely. The left hip is raised. An alternative direction is to move one foot forward obliquely while the other is drawn away in Sarna and they are placed one tala apart. One hand is in Lata while the other is placed on the hip. The Sukatunda hands are bent and placed on the chest and then slowly lowered down.

Avalokita : To look downwards.

Avarta : One foot in Kuncita should be put forward and them turned round quickly. The hands should be moved in harmony. The Dola hands are moved in Udvestita and Apavestita. The right foot performs Janita, Sakasasya and Urudvrtta while the left performs Nikusttaka, Prsthapasarpi and Casagati. The hips are turned round. The left foot Prsthapasarpi.

Avartita Movement : The belly is moved. To move the shanks in Avartita, the left foot is moved to the left repeatedly.

Avetita Karana : The fingers, beginning from the forefinger, are moved inward.

Aviddha : One Kuncita foot is moved out from Svastika and stretched. Then it falls on the ground in Ancita. The eyes look upwards and downwards.

Aviddhavakra : The hands are moved gracefully with the arms, the elbows and the shoulders. The palms of the hands are turned back. The hands are moved in various ways.

Aviddhavartana : The Aviddhavakra hands are moved in Vyavartita alternately and then they form Aviddha.

Avikriya : A still glance.

Avyaja : A clear look.

Ayata : The dancer stands in Catnrasra with her feet placed nine inches apart. Her knees are a little bent, obliquely. The left foot is placed normally in Sarna while the other is placed obliquely one tala apart. The chest is raised and the hands in Lata are placed on the hips. The dancer has a pleasing expression. Alternatively, the right foot is placed in Sarna while the left is placed obliquely. The left hip is raised.

Abhidrava : Insolenc.

Abhighata : Attack.

Abhighatasam : Accidental of violent attack.

Abhijit : Vega.

Abhilasa : Longing.

Abhinaya : Indication through gestures and verbal representation.

Abhinetris : Actress.

Abhiplutartham : Want of Synthesis.

Abhipraya : Fancy, Opinion.

Abhisarika : One who approaches the husband.

Abhitapta : Distressed.

Abhraca : Mica.

Abhutaharana : Mis-statement.

Adbhuta : Mysterious, Wonderment.

Adhama : Inferior.

Adhibala : Out vying, Outwitting.

Adhisthanas : Bases.

Adhomukha : Kept downwards.

Adhyavasaya : Perseverance.

Aho : Ah, How Wonderful.

Ahrdyaapriyaveksa : Seeing what is unwholesome or disple-asing.

Aksara : Syllable.

Aksara Sanghata : Compact, Non-brevity.

Alaktaka Raga : Red-lace.

Alamkaras : Figures of speech, Embellishments.

Alata : After Alata Cari the hand is taken down from the level of the Shoulder.

Alatacakra : Fire brand.

Alpa : Weak, Sparing.

Alpatva : Deficiency.

Alpatva and **Bahutva :** Reduction and amplification of notes.

Amarsa : Anger, Indignation.

Amba : Mother.

Amsa : Part, Key note.

Anabhyasa : Non repetition.

Ananaddha : Covered.

Anavasthita : Unsteady.

Ancita : In the Ardhasvasstika the Karihasta alternately in Vyarvartita and Parivarti.

Angaracana : Painting the limbs of the body.

Anidra : Sleeplessnes Animesapreksana Staring with winkless eyes.

Anista : Unfavourable.

Anista Sravana : Hearing seeing and discussing what is Darsana Pariki undesirable.

Antara Svara : Transitional note, Intermediate notes.

Antara : Transitional.

Antasthas : Semi vowels.

Anubandha : Continuity.

Anubandhaja : Growing out of mere succession.

Anubhavas : Consequents.

Anucarika : Attendant woman.

Anudatta : Grave.

Anukta Siddhi : Unattained achievement.

Anulapa : Repeated utterance.

Anumana : Deduction.

Anunaya : Imploring Mediation.

Anunasikyas : Nasal Sounds.

Anurupa : Befitting, Natural.

Anusmrts : Recollection.

Anusvara : Harmonious note.

Anuvrtta : Following up.

Anuvvdi : Assonant.

Anga Vicestitas : Movements of the limbs.

Angada : Amaband.

Angaharas : Major dance figure.

Angaja : Provoked by the limbs.

Angamadhuryam : Charm of the limbs, Components.

Anguli Vikepa : Throwing up gesture with the fingers.

Anka : Act

Ankamukha : Anticipatory Scene.

Ankavatara : Transitional Scene.

Ankura : Shoot.

Apada : Having no foot.

Apadesa : Statement.

Apahasita : Osbcene laughter.

Apakranta : Make the Valita thigh and perform Apakranta Cari both the hands to be moved in harmony.

Apakrsta : Yatis and the panis are dragged on by the arrangement of syllables.

Apalapa : Change of words.

Aparudita : Crying out of tune.

Apasmara : Loss of memory.

Apasrta : Withdrawn slightly.

Apavada : Censure.

Apavtiritaka : Concealed speaking.

Apaviddha : The right hand in Sukatunda gesture falls on the thigh, the left hand kept.

Apadana : Separating.

Apoha : Negative reasoning.

Apradaksina Pravesa : Entering clockwise or anticlockwise.

Aranya Pravesa : Entering a forest.

Ardha Mukta : Partially liberate.

Ardhahasa : Smile.

Ardhamatalli : Feet drawn away from the position in the Skhalita, left hand and later part on the hip.

Ardhamukula : Half bud

Ardhanikuttaka : Hands with Alapallava gesture bent towards shoulderse and legs moved up and down.

Ardhapani : Half-handed.

Ardharecita : Hand with Sucimukha gestures moves freely, feet move up and down in turns side in Sannata posture.

Ardhasama : Semi even.

Ardha Suci : The Alapadma hand is held on the head, right foot in Suci Karana.

Ardhasvastika : The two feet make Svastika, righthand Karihasta gesture left one lying on the chest.

Ardha Nigrhita : Semi lrrested.

Ardhardhapani : Quarter handed.

Argala : Feet stretched backwards and kept two Talas and a half a part. Hands moved in confonnity.

Arka : Sun.

Arpana : Presentation.

Artha : Wealth, Monetary help.

Artha Prakrti : Elements of the plot.

Artha Srngara : Love actuated by profit motivet.

Arthahinam : Meaningless want of significance.

Arthavyakti : Clarity of meaning, Directness of Expression.

Arthdntaram : Conveying another sense, superfluous expre-ssion.

Arthdpatti : Presumption.

Asammoha : Composure and absence of infatuation.

Asamyuta : Non combined.

Asatpralapa : Incoherent chatter.

Astravit : Expert in missiles.

Asuya : Jealousy, Envy.

Asitas : Brownish in colour.

Asru : Shedding tears.

Asvasthakdmita : One afflicted by uneasy and concealed love.

Asvins : Physicians of the Devas.

Atibhass : Superhuman language.

Atidesa : Agreement.

Atihasa : Boisterous laughter.

Atijagati Metre : Thirteen syllables.

Atikranta : Observe Atikranta Cari, stretch both the hands forward in a manner befitting the dance.

Atikrti: Twenty five syllables.

Atiprasanga : Prolixity.

Atsakkvari : Fifteen syllables.

Atsaya (Gunatisya) : Excellence.

Atusukya : Impatient curiosity.

Audarya : Nobility.

Audavitikrta : Pentatonic.

Auddrya : Dignity, Exalted State.

Audavikarana : Pentatonic treatment.

Augrya : Ferocity.

Autsukya : Yearning.

Avaddta : Cultured and refined.

Avahittha : Dissimulation.

Avahitthaka : After employing janita Karana raise the hands. Spreading out the fingers and Let them fall slowly.

Avakrasta : Low.

Avalagita : Transference.

Avalokita : Looking down.

Avannddha : Instrument of percussion.

Avanaddha Varga : Orchestra of covered instruments.

Avaroha : Descending.

Avaspandita : Ominons Significance.

Avastai : Condition.

Avasthas : Stages, Situations.

Avinasi : Imperishable.

Avite : There.

Avyatuita : Bereft.

Atikrti : Twenty five syllables.

Ayatnaja Alamkara : Graces not forced.

Ayatnajas : Effected easily, Even involuntary.

Ayuks : Odd ones.

Abharonakrt : Goldsmith, Maker of ornaments.

Abhrana : Jewellery.

Abhugna : Bent slightly.

Abhyantara : Internal exclusive, Regular, Conforming to the rules.

Acamana : Ceremonial rinsing of the mouth.

Adana : Summing up.

Adhikarika : The main one, The principal theme.

Agamas : Tradition treaties.

Aharya : Embellishment through dress & ornaments etc.

Ahvana : Beckoning.

Akasa Bhasita : Speaking to the sky. Addressing some one not presents.

Akasiki : Aerial.

Akekara : Half-close.

Akhyata : Verbal forms.

Aksiptarecita : Left hand on the heart right hand Recita, thrown up and sideways, then both the hand Recita with Apundha gesture.

Aksepa : Casual.

Aksepiki : Indicating.

Aksipta : Revelation, Hands and feet thrown about swiftly.

Alasya : Lethargy.

Alapa : Accosting.

Aloka and **Loka :** Speacial Mountains of twilight.

Alokita : Seeing over.

Amukha : Introduction.

Amukhangas : Ancillaries of Amukha.

Ananda : Joy.

Anandaja : Born of delight.

Angika : Gestures from the limbs.

Arabhati : Vigorous physical activity, Energetic or impetous one. Energetic Style.

Aroha : Ascending scale.

Arohi : Ascending.

Aropya : Put around.

Aryabhasa : Langauge of the Nobility.

Aryaputra : Noble one's son.

Asana : Sitting posture.

A sarita : Showering of flowers on the stage.

Asthapita Srogara : Stabilized love.

Asyaraga : Colour of the face.

Ascaryavadabhi : Telling tales of surprise khyanam.

Atmagata : Speaking to oneself.

Atmastha : Self-based, Personal.

Atmavan : Self-possessed, Prudent.

Atmopaksepakrtam : Made Through self reproach.

Atmosha : One's own.

Atodya : Instrumental music, Musical instrument.

Avapata : Commotion.

Avarta : Some kind of circular mark, the Kuncita feet put forward, two hands moved swiftly to befit the dancing.

Avaha : Marriage ceremony at the groom's place.

Avahana : In vocation.

Avedhya : Limbs are pierced and worn.

Avega : Excitement, Agitation.

Aviddha : Crooked, Aggressive, Breaking up.

Ayatatva : Tenseness of strings.

Ayuktika : Female supervisors.

Ayusman : Long lived.

Ancita : Use, the head is turned back.

★★★★★

Bhanda : Gourd etc. Shaped like Vessels.

Bhara : Burden.

Bharati Vrtti : Verbal style Verbal Utterance.

Bhasana : Clever speech.

Bhasyas : Glosses.

Bhava : Honoured sir, Feeling.

Bhava Natya : Dramatic art and gesticulation of emotions.

Bhava of **Hela :** Sportive passion.

Bhavagrahi : Capable of regaining lost love.

Bhavas : Sensitive feelings, Emotional fervour and state.

Bhavayanti : Fully compelend and pervade, Instill meaning.

Bhavita : Pervaded assimilated.

Bheda : Dissension, Incitement.

Bhedana : Piercing.

Bhindi : Javelin.

Bhinnartham : Conveying different meaning.

Bhogavati : Where in the first fourth and the last are long.

Bhogini : Mistress.

Bhramana : Circular movement.

Bhramaraka : Svastika feet in Aksipta Carid, hands in Udvestita. The sacrum turned round.

Bhramaramala : The metre in which the first two and the last two syllables are Guru.

Bhramari : The dancer performs the Atikranta Cari and turns her hips round. She moves round on her other foot.

Bhramita : Moving the wrist around.

Bhramsa : Lapse, slip of the tongue.

Bhranta : The eyelids are moved.

Bhrantapadancia : The dancer turns round her right foot and supports the left shank by the back of the right to. Then she performs Ancita. She touches the ground with her shoulders and turns round sideways waving headset.

Bhranti : Error.

Bhrarnari : The dancer stretches her foot and moves round quickly.

Bhrukutti : To raise the inner end of the eyebrows.

Bhugna : The mouth is slightly open.

Bhujanga Trastarecita : Feet in Bhujnga Traxita Cari hands Recita to be moved to the left.

Bhujanga Trtisita : One foot in Kuncita is thrown up and one thigh is moved obliquely. The hips and the knees are also moved. The left hand is raised and then bent in Khatikamukha. The right hand points downwards.

Bhujangancita : The feet in Bhujangatracita Cari right hand Recita, left hand Lata gestur. The right foot is in Bhujangatracita. The right hand is moved in Recita and the left hand is in Lata. The right hand is placed on the hips in Ancita.

Bhujanga Trastarecita : First Bhujangatracita is to be performed. Then the hands in Recita should be moved to the left side of the dancer.

Bhujangi : The dancer repeats the movement of the Simhi Gati with her hands in Tripataka on both sides.

Bhumi : Ground.

Bhumikas : Various roles, Different roles.

Bhusna : Ornaments.

Bhutas : Living beings spirits.

Bibhatsa Movement : The eyelids are contracted at the corners.

Bibhtitsa : Odious.

Bija : Seed, Main plot, Germ of the theme.

Bimboka : Affected coldness, Feigned anger.

Bindu : Turning point, The nucleus, Prominent point.

Bisa : The dancer places her feet on the ground and then she jumps.

Brahma : Lord of the worlds, Self-born lord, Grand-father.

One foot is in Sarna while the other is moved back in Kuncita and then thrown up keeping the knee joint straight.

Brsi : Seat made of grass.

Bruhi : Hell.

★★★★★

Caitra : Surabhi Month.

Cakita Movement : A restless glance.

Cakra Bandha : The dancer moves her hands, arms and feet. This is done to four to six talas, one after the other, some fast, some slow, having a regular beat.

Cakrabhramari : The dancer spins like a wheel in the middle of Khanda Suci and her hands m Tripataka.

Cakrakuttanika : One foot in Nikuttana is turned round from the side followed by a normal Nikuttana.

Cakra Mandala : The hands hang down and the body is bent in. The hands are placed on the thighs with the right hand bent. The dancer spins like a wheel. The inner Apaviddha (Addita Cari) with the body bent and held down between, the two arms hanging straight.

Cakravaka : Ruddy gheese.

Cala : Nikunca and Akuncita are done one after the other repeatedly.

Cala Movement : The glance quickly look at everything.

Calana : The dancer walks. Trembling movement.

Calita Movement : The thighs are moved.

Camatkaranrtya : The hands are joined and the dancer dances to the accompaniment of the Aksaras.

Candrakanta : One hand assumes Makara after performing Ardhacandra while the other hand assumes Sukatunda. Then both the hands touch the knee and move up to touch the head.

Candravarta : One foot is raised at the side to touch the ear and the dancer moves slowly in Bhramarika holding her big toe with her hand.

Cankramana : The dancer moves in jumps with the outer sides of her feet.

Capalata : Inconstancy, Fickle mindedness, Restlessness.

Casagati : The right foot is extended and then drawn away. The left foot is also drawn away.

Casaka : Sarhyutahasta. Puspaputa hands are joined at the elbows.

Catu : The dancer tuches the ground with her knees and describes a circle with her legs. Her hands are in Lata and she revolves.

Catula Movement : To look at a disagreeable object.

Catunnukhalohadi : Lohadi is done turning to all four sides.

Catura : Ingeniously adroit. The left hand is in Ancita while the right hand is in Catura. The right foot moves up and down. To move the eyebrows in a pleasing manner. Very clever, Excellent, right feet in Kuttita pose.

Caturasra : Square in shape. The feet placed eighteen angulas apart. The Khatakamukha hands are held forward eight fingers apart from each other on the breasts. The shoulders are on the same level. Four stringed.

Caturasrakhyavartana : The Caturasra hands are moved along with the shoulders and elbows. The arms first assume Udvestita and then placed on the chest.

Caturka : Four some.

Caturthakara : Fourth Man.

Catuskonanikuttita : Nikuttana is done in front and at the back. This is repeated thrice.

Catuspada : Four footed.

Catuspatrabja : One hand is raised at first and it describes a circle. Then it is stretched to all the four side while the other hand rests on the navel.

Cencalagati : The first the fifth and last syllables are long.

Cestakrta : Brought about by the movements.

Cetas : Menials and personal attendants.

Chadana : Concealment.

Chala : Deception.

Chandovit : One conversant with prosody.

Chedana : Cutting. The motion of cutting.

Cheva : The dancer expresses emotions with the corners of her eyes and the eyebrows.

Chinna : The Alapadma hand to be held on the hip in Chinna pose, Body in the Vaisakha sthana. The teeth are finally pressed together and Turned aside.

Chinna Movement : To turn the middle of the hips around.

Cinta : Anxiety .

Citra : The dancer mostly moves in the Tiryanmukha Gati. Variegated, Portrait.

Citra Abhinaya : Special Representation.

Citra Movements of Shanks : To move up and clown bending the toe gracefully .

Citra Bhramari : The dancer stands in the pose of Trivikrama and turns to the left.

Citrakrt : Painter.

Cudamani : Crest jewel.

Cukkita : The position of the chin when the mouth is wide open.

Culika : Informatory speech.

Curna Pada : Prose, Simple Steps.

Curnas : Prose.

★★★★★

Daha : Burning sensation.

Dainya : Depression, Dejection, Wretchedness.

Daiviki : Divine.

Daksina : Dexterous. Monetary gift.

Daksinya : Clever manners, Chivalry.

Damari : The dancer makes circualr movements at the right and the left sides with one foot which is bent.

Damarukuttita : One foot is placed in Nikuttana after which the toes are dragged.

Dana : Striking.

Danda : Beam, Chastisement, Baton.

Danda Pada : The dancer crosses her feet in Svastika and throws them up obliquely. The feet are extended in Dandapada after performing Nupura. The Aviddhavakra is performed quickly. The hands are in Aviddha and placed straight like a staff. The right foot performs Janita and Dandapada successively while the left foot performs Suci. The hips are turned round. Then the right foot performs Udvrtta, Parsvakranta. Bhujangatrasita and Danda pada successively and the left foot performs Alata, Atikranta and Suci successively.

Dandakarecita : Hands and feet freely thrown about all sides like a staff and then Recita.

Dandapaksa : Having performed Urdhvajanu Lata hands should be plasced on the knees. The Harpsapaksa hands move alternately and then stretch out like a staff.

Dandapranamancita : The dancer jumps as she does in Ancita and comes down on the ground straight as a staff.

Dandavartana : The Dandapaska hands are rotated round.

Dantu : The dancer performs Sulu, places one foot forward and crosses it with the other.

Darpasarana : The dancer stands in the Vaisanava Sthana and falls to the ground sideways.

Dasagati : Menials, Servants.

Data : The lower lip is pressed by the teeth.

Desa : Locality.

Desabhasa : Local language.

Desi gata : Those of native origin.

Desikara : A sequence of refined movements which avoid anything coarse or vulgar.

Deva : Lord.

Devas : Venerable ones.

Devasila : Divine type.

Devata : Deity.

Devis : Dancers in the guise of goddesses.

Devopaharaka : The Arala hands are moved at both sides. One hand is stretched out while the other points at the elbow.

Dhairya : Bravery.

Dhaivata : Right hand.

Dhala : The dancer moves her body like the movement of a drop of water on a lotus. This is also known a Tana.

Dhanad : Kubera.

Dhanurakarsana : The Svastika hands are quickly and obliquely brought to the sides. One hand touches the ear.

Dhanurvallivinamaka : The hands are raised near the head, the hips and at the sides with palms turned downwards.

Dhara : Current.

Dharma : Piety.

Dharma Srngara : Love based on piety.

Dharmi : Rehearsed, Practice.

Dharstya : Impudence.

Dhenki : The dancer jumps and moves both feet together from one side to the other.

Dhi : Intelligence.

Dhillai : A dance of soft movements performed with Sausthava and full of Bhava and Hela.

Dhira : A majestic glance. Bold.

Dhrti : Fortitude, Confirmation.

Dhruva : To keep still.

Dhruva Pravesiki : Entering.

Dhruvanrcya : The dancer moves her body and hands in Avestita and Hastakaranas. She begins from the right side and gradually moves to the centre of the stage. She performs hand gestures and dances to Dhruva.

Dhunana : Shaking. To shake.

Dhurta : Cheat, Rogue, Gamesters.

Dhuta : Slow movement of the head.

Dhuvada : The dancer performs Bhramari at the beginning and at the end of the performance. She does three Sulus near her breasts and performs Bhujangatrasita.

Digbhramari : The dancer moves as in Sirobhramari except that she first revolves on the one side, then on the other. Then she touches the ground with her hand and revolving on her arm moves successively in four directions.

Digvarsabhidhacalana : The hands are moved to the front, at the sides and at the back. They are also raised and moved obliquely.

Diksvastika : The hands and the feet are placed in Svastika in front or at the sides of the dancer. Turning sideways and towards the front in course of a connected movement.

Dina : Piteous. The lower eyelid is slightly lowered, then pupils are still and full of tears and they move slowly.

Dindu : The dancer jumps with both feet, moves round and jumps again. The dancer stands in Sarna, then she jumps to the front and sits and moves round her body bending to the front.

Dipaka : Illumination through condensed, Expression.

Dipana : Brightening, Brilliance.

Dipita : First and the fifth are short and the rest are long.

Dipta : Excited, Illuminated.

Dipti : Radiance.

Dista : Description.

Divya : Divine, Fascinating.

Divya Manusa : Semi divine.

Divyadarsana : Seeing a heavenly being.

Dodhaka : Cub of an elephant.

Dola : Each hand is moved up and down obliquely in a graceful way. This is done alternately. The shoulders are slackened and the hands are let down in Pataka.

Dolana : To swing.

Dolapada : Kuncita foot thrown up two hands swinging from side to side in a manner befitting the dance. The hands are moved in harmony. The palms are shown.

Dosas : Defects.

Dosoda Harana : Pointing out the faults of others.

Drapta : Haughty, Arrogant.

Drdhvajanu : The dancer raises her Kuncita foot to touch the breast with the knee and shakes it.

Drdhvalaga : The dancer comes down after jumping and Praises her feet in Sarna. The dancer sits down and performs Dindu. Then she performs Alaga with her face raised.

Drpta Movement : The pupils are motionless and the eyes are wide open. This steady glance shows firmness.

Drstanata : Precedent.

Drsti : Peculiar look, Vision, Glance.

Drstivyakosa : Opening the eyes wide.

Drstyakuncana : Contracting the eyes Duhkha Sorrow.

Druta : Quick, Rapid, Fast.

Drutacapala : In the foot of a metre there are eighteen Syllables.

Drutalaya : Quick tempo.

Drutall : Quick.

Duhsila : Ill-natured.

Duracara : Ill-doing, Tyrant.

Duta : Messenger.

Duti : Meaning fully.

Dvara Parsva : The sides of the entry way.

Dvikalas : Having only two Kalas.

Dvipada : Two footed.

Dvisankhyata : Doubled in number.

Dvisara : Two stringed.

Dvisikhara : Both the hands are in Sikhara.

Dyuti : Rebuke.

★★★★★

Earma : Shiel.

Ekacarnancita : Ancita is done with one foot.

Ekadesaja : Partia.

Ekajanunata : One foot is in Sama while the other foot is kept obliquely with the knee bent and placed at a distance of four angulas from the Sarna foot.

Ekapada : One leg is in Sarna with the knee raised. The other foot touches the outer side of the knee with its own outer side.

Ekapada Bhramari : The dancer revolves alternately on one foot.

Ekapada Kuttita : One foot performs Nikuttana at its own side with the toes followed by similar movements of the other foot.

Ekapada Lohadi : This Lohadi done with one foot. It is also described as Ekapadalunthita.

Ekaparsvagata : One foot is placed obliquely touching the ground with its outer edge in front of the other foot which is in Sarna.

Ekatalinrtya : The dancer dances in a fast tempo to Ekatala. Bhramarikas are performed in between the Calakas. Kalasas and Lasyangas are performed.

Ekocca : One shoulder is raised.

Elakakridita : Jump with Talasancara feet and come to the ground with the body bent and turned. The hands are in Kuncita and Recita. The hips are quickly turned round. Then she moves round in Sucividdha and Apaviddha successively.

Enapluta : The dancer jumps and performs Suci in the air. Then she comes down to the ground and performs Utkatasana above the ground.

★★★★★

Gaccha : Go.

Gadgada : Choked voice.

Gajadanta : The hands touch the opposite arms between the shoulders and elbrows. Left hand bent and brought near the left ear, right hand in Lata gesture. Dolapada is then performed. The right leg is placed at the back while the right hand is put forward. The left leg points upward.

Gajalila : The dancer stands in Samapada and moves slowly with a grave look.

Gambhirya : Gravity.

Ganakas : Reckoners.

Ganas : Attendants.

Ganda : Undue combination of words.

Ganda Suci : The feet are in Suci. One side is bent. One hand is placed on the chest and the other touches the cheek in a curve. One foot is in Agratalasancara while, the right is bent.

Gandhara : The dancer looks with Karuna Drsti, bends her head and moves her Sukatunda hand.

Gandharava : Musician.

Gandhdra : No finger, Fully open.

Gangavatarana : The feet are raised with the soles turned up. The hands are turned down in Tripataka and the head is bent.The left leg is raised while the left hand is in Recita. The chest is raised.

Garbha : Development.

Garhana : Censure.

Garuda : The Ardhacandra hands are placed obliquely to touch the thumbs. The left leg bends forward slightly while the other touches the ground at the back.

Garuda Bhramari : The dancer stretches one foot obliqulely, touches the ground with the other knee and revolves with her hands stretched out.

Garudapaska : The hands should be placed on the hips with their palms slightly bent and facing downwards.

Garudapluta : The feet are extended backward. One hand is in Lata and the other is in Recita. The head is raised. The feet are placed in Vrscika and Breast is raised.

Garva : Arrogance, Pride.

Gatagata : The dancer, after raising one of her feet hesitates to move.

Gati : Movements.

Gati Mandala : Angahara, Mandalasvastika, Nivesa, Unmatta, Udghattia, Mattalli; Aksipta, Uromandala and Katicchinna Karanas are used. The dancer performs Mandalasthanaka, and then places the hands in Recita,the feet in Udghattita. The Angahara is ended by performing Mattalli, Aksipta, Uromandala and Katicchinna.

Gatipracara : Taking steps.

Gatis or **Pravicaras :** Mode of walking or movements.

Gativrtti : Tempo

Gatravartana : The hands in Alapallava are moved inwards in Vyavrtta and then, placed back to back they assume Alapallava.

Gaura : Wheatish Brown, Pale Red.

Gayana : Singer.

Gayatri : Six syllables.

Geya : Song.

Geyapada : Sample song.

Ghana : Solid.

Gharghara : A performance done with Kinkinis is called Gharghara.

Ghatas : Inauspicious features.

Ghatavartana : The hands are moved in Udvetita.Then they are raised together from the chest and the shoulders and finally they are moved near the shoulders.

Ghattita Movements of Shanks : The dancer strikes the ground with her heels.

Ghosa : Sound of musical instrument.

Ghurnita : Left hand in Valita and moved round, right hand with Dola gesture and the two feet to be drawn away from each other from the Svastika position.

Gitam : Music.

Gitanrtya : The dancer performs with Sausthava the following talas and Varnas. The words are acted with the hands and Bhavas.

Gitavidhi : Application of the songs.

Giti : Rhythm.

Glana Movement : The eyebrows, the eyelashes and the eyelids droop. The eyes move slowly and feebly.

Gland : Languid, Fatigued, Weakness.

Gomaya : Dried cowdung.

Gopuccha : Cow's tail.

Gotraskhalita : Blunder in addressing.

Graha : Commencement.

Graha Mdrga : Way of beginning.

Gramas : Scales.

Granthima : Tied up.

Granthimatkesa : Made up of locks of hair Mukutas.

Grathana : Assembling.

Grdhravalinaka : One foot is extended backward. One knee is a little bent while the arms are stretched out. The feet are placed five talas apart, the hands are left down and the dancer looks to the front. The foot which is extended backward should touch the ground with its big toe and the hands should move in Lata.

Grisma : Summer.

Grivarecaka : The neck is raised, then lowered and then bent sideways. The neck is moved round.

Grivd : Neck.

Grivd Bhanga : Breaking of the neck.

Gromani : Leader of the groups.

Guccha : Bunch.

Gudhartha : Circulocution, Hidden meaning.

Guhyanam Guhanam : Concealment of the objects to be concealed.

Gunakirtana : Enumeration of merits, Glorification of the qualities of the lover.

Gunas : Excellence, Merits.

Gunatipata : Opposition to virtue, Accusation of virtues.

Gundala : The dancer revolves quickly in time with the beat and moves her shanks in and out.

Guru : Long.

★★★★★

Hamsapaksa : Three fingers are extended, the little is raised and the thumb is bent.

Ha Ha : Alas.

Hamsi : The dancer places her foot at a distance of half a cubit from the other and bending her body on both sides alternately, with her hands in Kapittha. The dancer moves like a swan with appropriate Bhavas. The dancer moves like a goose.

Hands represent planet Budha : Musti is shown in an oblique position by the left hand while the right hand is in Pataka.

Hands represent planet Candra : The left hand is in Alapadma and the right hand is in Patika.

Hands represent planet Guru : The sacred thread is indicated by the Sikhara hands. This gesture can also represent a Rsi or a Brahmin.

Hands represent planet Ketu : The left hand is in Suci and the right hand is in Pataka.

Hands represent planet Sani : The left hand is in Sikhara while the right hand is in Trisula.

Hands represent planet Sukra : Both the hands are in Musti and the left hand is raised while the right hand is lowered.

Hands represent planet Surya : The hands are placed near the shoulder in Alapadma and Kapittha.

Hands represent Agni : The right hand performs Tripataka while the left hand assumes Kailgula.

Hands represent Brahma : The left hand is in Catura and the right is in Harpsasya.

Hands represent Brahmana : The hands are in Sikhara and the right hand in an oblique position, include the sacred thread.

Hands represent caste Kastriya : The left hand in Sikhara, is placed obliquely while the right hand is in Pataka.

Hands represent Indra : Tripataka hands are crossed in Svastika.

Hands represent Isvara : The left hand is in Mrgasirsa while the right hand is in Tripataka.

Hands represent Kalki : The left hand is Tripataka while the right hand is in Pataka.

Hands represent Krsna : The hands perform Mrgasirsa together and are placed near the face.

Hands represent Kurma : Kurma hands are performed and then the hands are placed on the same level with the shoulders.

Hands represent Kuvera : The left hand is in Padma while the right hand is in Gada.

Hands represent Laksmi : The hands, in Kapittha, are placed near the shoulder.

Hands represent Manmatha : The left hand is in Sikhara and the right hand is in Khatakamukha.

Hands represent Matsya : The hands, after performing Matsya, are placed on the same level with the shoulders.

Hands represent Nirrti : Khattva and Sakata to be performed.

Hands represent Nrsirpha : The left hand is in Sirphamukha and the right hand is in Tripataka.

Hands represent Parasurama : The left hand is placed on the waist while the right hand performs Ardhapataka.

Hands represent Parvati : The right hand, in Ardhacandra, is raised and the left hand also in Ardhacandra, is lowered. The hands show dispel fears.

Hands represent planet Kuja : Tile left hand shows Suci and the right hand is in Pataka.

Hands represent Ramacandra : The right hand, in Kapittha, and the left hand, in Sikhara, are raised.

Hands represent relationship Dampati : The left hand is in Sikhara while the right hand is in Mrgasirsa.

Hands represent relationship Matr : The left hand is in Ardhacandra and the right hand is in Sandarpsa. Then the left hand is turned round and placed on the belly.

Hands represent relationship Nanandr : At the end of the Bhartrbhratr - hasta, the right hand shows a feminine gesture.

Hands represent relationship Pitr : The right hand of the Matrhasta assumes Sikhara.

Hands represent relationship Saptani : Mter performing the Pasahasta, both the hands make a feminine gesture.

Hands represent relationship Svasura : The right hand of the Svasruhasta is in Sikhara.

Hands represent Sanmukha : The left hand is in Trisula and the right hand, which is raised.

Hands represent Sarasvati : The right hand is in Suci while the left hand, in Kapittha, is raised near the shoulder.

Hands represent Valarama : The right hand is in Pataka while the left hand is in Musti.

Hands represent Vamana : The left hand, in Musti is raised and the right hand also in Musti, is lowered.

Hands represent Varaha : The hands are placed by the side of the waist after Varaha is performed.

Hands represent Varuna : The right hand is in Pataka and the left hand is in Sikhara.

Hands represent Vayu : The right hand is in Arala and the left hand is in Aradhapataka.

Hands represent Vinayaka : The Kapittha hands are placed near the shoulder.

Hands represent Visnu : Both the hands assume Tripataka .

Hands represent Yama : The left hand is in Pasa and the right hand is in Suci.

Hands representing caste Sudra : The left hand is in Sikhara and the right hand is in Mrgasirsa.

Hara : Chain.

Haradamavilasaka : The hands touch the opposite shoudlers and then they are lowered together at the sides.

Harilsakalasa : The dancer moves in different gaits like a swan with her hands in Harhsasya.

Harinapluta : After doing Atikranta the dancer jumps up, and on coming down she throws up her shanks which are bent. One foot performs the Atikranta Cari.

Harinatatrasika : The dancer crosses her Kuncita feet in Svastika and curves the foreparts of the soles. Then she jumps up and comes down.

Harita : Green.

Harpsasya : The forefinger, the middle finger and the thumb are closely joined in a triangular position. The two other fingers are extended.

Harsa : Delight, Serpent shaped ornament.

Harsta Movement : The pupils move in wards in the moving eyes which are slightly lowered and winking. They are full of joy.

Hasa : Merriment.

Hasita : Slight laughter.

Hasta : Hand.

Hastali and **Valaya :** Types of bangles.

Hastarecaka : The hands are raised, thrown out, extended, turned round and drawn backwards. A quick and circular movement of the Hamrhsapaksa hands, done alternately.

Hasya : Humorous, Comic.

Hasya Movement : The eyes are narrowed gradually and the moving.

Hava : Emotion.

Havya : Offerings into the fire.

Helav : Passion.

Hemanta : Early Winter.

Hetu : Causation.

Hetvavadharana : Ascertainment of the cause.

Hikaa : Hiccup

Hladi Movement : A glance that effaces all sorrows.

Hollu : The dancer moves from her breasts, her Lata hands to her back. She performs the Stambhakridanika Cari with other appropriate Caris.

Hora Movement : A harsh look.

Hormayi : The dancer makes Svastika with her feet and moves one backward. Then she crosses it with the other.

Hotr : Performer of sacrifice.

Hrllekha : Heartache, Grief anxiety.

Hrsta : Joyous.

★★★★★

Iccha : Wish.

leIstasya Arthasya : Expressing the desired object Vacanam.

Insult : Avamana.

Ipsitamanorathavapti : Attainment of the cherished desire .

Irsyakopaprayam : Full of acts of Jealousy and anger.

Ista : Favourab.

Itivrtta : Story, Plot.

Itu : This.

★★★★★

Jada : A feeble and still look.

Jadata : Stupor, Sluggishness.

Jakkadi : The dancer holds her veil. The dance is graceful and full of Bhramaris.

Jalasayana : The dancer after falling to the ground takes the pose of lying in water. She is placing the left palm on the ground, resting the head on the left palm and then lying down in one hip, one thigh and one shank. The other foot should be pointed up.

Janantika : Addressing particular person.

Jangha : Calf, Shank.

Janghavarta : The dancer throws up one foot, the sole of which is turned inwards, at the back of the knee, while she places at its side, the other foot, the sole of which is turned inwards.

Janita : One hand is placed on the chest in Musti while the other is moved round. One foot is moved round. The dancer stands on her toes. The legs are bent and so is the neck.

Japa : Recitation of holy name and utterance of pray.

Jarjara : Smashed to smithereens, Flagstaff.

Jata Mukuta : Crowns of matted hair.

Jatibhasa : Laguage of the laity.

Jatighalailghanika : The dancer kicks up one of her feet other which is slightly bent.

Jayanta : The left hand assumes Makara while the right assumes Ardhacandra. Then the left hand is moved and placed at the right in Pataka. The other hand in Tripataka is placed on the shoulder.

Jhampatala : The dancer dances in a "middle" tempo following a song sung to the Jhampatala. Kalasa and Lasyangas are performed with the hand gestures.

Jhasa : Fish.

Jihma Movement : The eyelids are lowered and slightly contracted.

Jihvyas : Cerebrals.

Jivita : The very life.

Jneya Bhyanukta : Semi-uttered, Expression.

Jugupsa : Disgust.

Jugupsita Movement : The eyelids are contracted and the pupils are hidden and the eyes turn away from what lies in front.

Jyeyestha : Long.

★★★★★

Kadamba : Asarhyutahasta. The fingers are joined to form a circle.

Kaisika : Capillary.

Kaisiki Vrtti : Graceful Style, Charming.

Kaivartana : The dancer joins her hands at the wrists and moves them gracefully to her left and right sides.

Kakapada : Incision in the skin.

Khaki : Crow like Ka.

Ksavartana : The Parsva Manadala hands are moved together or alternately at their own sides.

Ksya Vibhaga : Division of the zones

Kaku : Intonation.

Kakusvana : Emphatic mutter.

Kalaha : Quarel.

Kalahantarita : Keeping the palm of the hand a loof due to quarrel, One estranged due to quarrel with the lover.

Kalantara : Different Kala.

Kalapa : The hands are interlocked with the fingers separated and raised. The thumbs are kept out.

Kalavitikavinoda : The dancer performs the Cakrabhramari, Nihsanka, Dantu, Hormayi successively and finally she ends the performance with a jump.

Kalpanrtya : Karanas and Sthanakas are performed.

Kalpita : Conceit.

Kalusa : The eyes show tiredness.

Kalvinkavinoda : The hands are rotated one after the other over the head and the sides. They are moved quickly and beautifully up and down.

Kama : Passionate, Attachment, Love.

Kamala : The dancer moves her arm in various ways such as Alapallavavartana and keeps her hips, sides and head straight.

Kamatantra : Science of love, Science of Erotics.

Kamini : The metre is which the Laghu alternate with Gurus.

Kamopacara : Loving attention.

Kampana Movement : This is done by shake the thighs and moving the heels up and down. To make the lower lip tremble.

Kampita Movement : Quick and oblique movement of the hips. Trembling cheeks. Shivering, To move the head quickly up and down several times.

Kampita Movements of Shanks : To shake the shanks.

Kanapa : Kampana.

Kanci : Gridle.

Kancukiya Gatii : Chamber loin.

Kandikas : Parts.

Kanistha : Short.

Kanta Movement : To glance. Joy and pleasure, Arching the eyebrows.

Kantha : Throat. Neck.

Kanthosthya : Throat-labral.

Kanti : Splendour, Charm.

Kapalacurnana : The dancer stands in Saina and touches the ground with her forehead. Then she returns to her original position.

Kapalasparsana : The dancer bends forward and touches the ground with her forehead. This seems to be the same action as Kapalacurnana.

Kapatas : Deception.

Kapha : Phlegm.

Kapota : Dove coloured.

Karanguli : Movements of hands and feet bhramana.

Karakas : Such as object etc.

Karana : Lunar conjunction.

Karananeri : The dancer dances in Jhampatala to the sound of the Gopuccha. Her hands are in Alapallava.

Karanas : Parsvajanu, Urdhavajanu, Dandapaska, Talavilasita, Vidyudbhranta, Candravarta, Nisumbhita, Lalatatilaka and Latavrscika. She does these facing the left and the right after which she stands in the Alidha Sthana, Dance movements.

Karandava : Species of duck.

Kararekaratna : The hands move to the sides and then brought to the middle of the body. Then they are placed on the hips in Svastika and moved in Valavyajanacalana. Then form Vartana Svastika with the palms turned down. They are raised describing circles and brought down in Svastika. One hand touches the shoulder while the other is swung in Rathacakra. Then they are stretched straight, raised and bent. Then they are again brought to the shoulders with a circular motion and then moved out to the front after doing this, they are moved up and down alternately from the head to the hips. The elbows crossed in Svastika rotated inward and outward.

Karasparsana : The dancer performe the Alaga Karana and touches the ground with her hands and revolves in a low position.

Karihasta : One hand is placed on the chest and the other moves in Udvestita. One foot is in Aficita. The left foot moves back while the right foot moves forward. The left hand is bent and placed on the hips. One hand is raised in Lata and swung on either side and another hand in Tripataka is held at the ear. The dancer rubs the ground with the sides of her feet.

Karkata : The fingers are interlocked.

Karnaculikas : Ear ornaments.

Karnayugmaprakirnaka : The hands are moved obliquely and alternately upto the ears and then they are brought to the sides and to tile front.

Karsya : Thinness, Weakness.

Kartari : The dancer jumps on her toes with one hand in Kartari placed the left foot and the other hand in Sikhara is placed on the hips pointing downward. The dancer performs the Uruveni Gati and other appropriate Gatis. The hands are moved near the chest and the Laghusekhara-Sulus are performed. The dancer stands facing different directions each time. The dancer quickly moves to the left and the right with her shanks crossed in Svastika.

Kartaridindu : The dancer performs Kartari and Hormayi.

Kartari Lohadi : This is Lohadi performed with the feet crossed in Svastika.

Kartaryancita : The dancer performs Ancita with her feet crossed in Svastika.

Karu : Craftsman.

Karuna Movement : The eyes are focused towards the nose with drooping lids.

Kasama Movement : To flatten the belly.

Kasaya : Dark Red.

Kastam : How pathetic.

Kat : Hip.

Katara Movement : A helpless look.

Kathodghata : Opening of the story.

Kati : Hip.

Katibhhranta : The right foot is placed on one side of the body after removing the left foot quickly. The hips are moved in Recita. Having performed Suci with the left foot, it is quickly drawn away. The right foot is placed on the right side of the body.

Katibhranti : The Suci Cari, Apaviddha gesture with the right hand, hip to be moved round.

Katichinna : The hands are repeatedly placed on the head in Pallava. The dancer stands in the Mandalasthana and moves her sides round. The hip serially in the Chinna position, two pallava hands held alternately. and repeatedly on the head.

Katinikuttaka : The hands are arched, one on the chest and the other on the hips, while the dancer looks downward and the rest are in Nikutta.

Katirecaka : The hips are raised, turned round and drawn backwards. The hips are turned in all directions with oblique movement of the separated and spread out toes.

Katirecaka : The feet are moved in Nikutta while the hands are in Lata. The hips are moved round.

Katisama : Feet kept separated after Svastika Karana one hand placed at the navel and the other at the hip side in the Udvahita pose. The feet are separated from Svastika. The side is raised.

Kaukkuti : The dancer moves her feet together like an excited cock.

Kavyaja : Provoked by words.

Kavyaja Hasya : Laughter due to words.

Kavyas : Poetical and dramatic compositions.

Kavyasamhara : Tennination

Kesabandha : Hair knot. The hands should move upwards from the two sides to touch the hair and back.

Kesabandhavartana : The Kesabandha hands are brought away from the hair alternately.

Keyura : Armlet

Khadgavartana : One hand in Musti moves in Kuncita while the other hand in Khatakamukha moves in Ancita.

Khalu-hula : The dancer stamps the ground with the heel of her left foot touching the ground with the forepart of the sole and moves round to the left and the right.

Khalva Movement : To flatten the belly.

Khanda Suci : One leg is in Kuncita. The other is stretched obliquely touching the ground with its knee and heel.

Khandita : Enraged.

Khanjani : The dancer bends her knees with her hands in Tripataka and moves round quickly with the foreparts of her feet and stops.

Khanjrita : The dancer moves like a bird.

Khatakamukhavartana : The wrists are moved to the left and the right of the body and near the navel.

Khatakavardhamanaka : One Khataka hand is placed on another Khataka hand.

Khatana : The action of the chin upon pressing the teeth together.

Kheda : Lassitude.

Khetaka : Riders shield.

Khutta : The dancer strikes the ground with her toes.

Kila : Ear Tops.

Kilakincitam : Hysterical Mood.

Kim : What.

Kincitsadrasi : Partial likeness.

Kintu : A dance in which movements of the eyebrows, breasts and hips follow.

Kirita : Sarhyutahasta. Kalapa is done above the head.

Kiriti : Crowned.

Koladiricindu : Alapa is done with a series of letters which bring out the meaning and has no tala. It is done in Pataraga.

Komala Movement : A graceful and calm look.

Komalika : The dancer moves round and performs Angananga thus indicating a soft heart.

Krama : Progress.

Kramapadanikuttika : This is done with both feet.

Kranta : The hands are thrown down. The hands assume Khatikamukha. One side is bent and the feet are in Recita. One leg is bent on the ground in the Atikranta Cari. One hand is moved away in Vyavrtta and then it is again moved away in Parivartita. The same hand is placed on the chest in Khatakamukha. The action is repeated by the other side of the body.

The right foot performs Suci and Parsvakranta while the left foot performs Apakranta and Parsvakranta. The dancer moves round performing these Caris alternately.

Krantaka : Bending a Kuncita leg behind the back and the Atikrimta Cari both the hands thrown down.

Kratasauca : Woman of inviolated chastity.

Kriya : Activity.

Krodha : Fury, Anger.

Krpalaga : The dancer touches her hips alternately with both heels and between them, places her hands in Ardhacandra.

Krsna : Black.

Krsnnta : Fate.

Krsya : Likely to be drawn.

Kruddha : Angry.

Kruddha Movement : An angry glance with the eyelashes still and the eyes raised. The pupils are motionless and fixed upwards. The eyebrows are knitted.

Ksama : The cheeks are depressed.

Ksanas : Moments.

Ksetrancita : With her feet in Ancita, the dancer sits in Utkatasana at the beginning and at the end of the movement.

Ksipta : Thrown out.

Ksipta Movements of Shanks : The shanks are thrown outwards.

Ksobhaja : Agitated.

Kudupa : The dancer trembles and extends her shank quickly with her big toe stretched out while the rest of the toes are curved.

Kufrcita : To narrow the eyelids.

Kulaka : Talaka

Kumaradhikrtas : The tutors and wardens of the princes.

Kumari : Virgin

Kumbha Bhedana : Breaking the pot.

Kumbhipadaka : Special tattoo mark.

Kunana : The action of the chin upon grinding the teeth.

Kuncanmula : Bent at the root.

Kuncita : Contracted.

Kuncita Movement : The eyelashes and the eyelids are slightly contracted and the pupils are completely contracted. The cheeks are contracted, The neck is curved, The right foot and the right hand are bent. The same and is turned upward and placed on the left side. The right leg touches the ground while the left leg is bent. The right hand is raised and placed on the left side in

Alapadma. The feet are in Agratalasancara. The toes are curved. To bend the eyebrows slightly together or one after the other.

Kuncita Movement of Knee : The shanks or thighs touch each other.

Kuncita Movements of Shanks : The dancer raises her heels, contracting her toes and arching her insteps.

Kuncita Bhramari : The dancer bends her knees and revolves.

Kundala : The ear ornament that hangs down suspended, Ear ring.

Kundalicara : The hands are moved to the left right and to all sides.

Kunta : Spear.

Kupla Movement : The eyes are frowning.

Kurmalaga : The dancer assumes Kurmasana while performing Alaga.

Kurmasana : The right leg touches the ground with the knee and the outer side of the ankle. The left foot is in Sarna. The left repeats the action of the right.

Kurmavatara : The hands are placed together or one after the other on the right and the left near the head. They are rotated and crossed in Svastika. They describe a large circle.

Kusala : Clever.

Kusilavas : Musicians.

Kutapa : Stringed instruments.

Kutila : Oblique.

Kuttamita : Pretended Anger.

Kuttana : The dancer stamps the ground with the heels or the foreparts or the soles of her feet.

★★★★★

Lagadindu : The dancer jumps in the air.

Lagapata : Both the feet are shaken delicately in the air.

Laghu : Short.

Laghu Kutai : Umbrella.

Laharicakrasundara : One hand is moved obliquely near the navel. The other hand is upturned and moved up to the left shoulder and stretched out. Then they are moved to the left and right side of the head and then gently brought down.

Lajjanvita Movement : The eyelashes are slightly contracted and the upper eyelids are lowered in shyness. Bashful.

Laksmi : Goddess of fortune.

Laksyate : Recognized.

Lalatatilaka : One foot moves in Vrscika and with its big toe a tilaka is marked on the forehead. The left foot touches the forehead.

Lalita Movement : Lollig, Sportiveness, Graceful, Left hand in Karihasta gesture and right hand turned aside (Apavartita) two feet moved. Lustful Lalita : One foot in Suci either strikes the other or it is kept apart. The left hand is in Karihasta. The right hand is moved round. One foot is repeatedly moved up and down. The Pallava hands are moved over the head. The eyes are narrowed at the corners. The eyebrows are knitted .The eyes are opened at the corners. The eyes lre slowly opened expressing affection.

Lalitabhinaya : Graceful movements.

Lalitagati : The fifth and the last syllables are long.

Lalitasancara : The right foot performs Urdhvajanu and Suci successively. The left foot performs Apakranta and the right foot is moved to the side. Again the left foot performs Suci and the hips are turned round. Then the right foot performs Parsvakranta, Suci and again Parsvakranta while the left foot does Atikranta, Apakranta. Parichinna is performed with Bahyabhramaraka.

Lalitavartana : The hands in Lalita are moved to the head and then each touches the tip of the other's fingers and move near the head in Khatakamukha.

Langhitajanghika : The dancer stands in the Khandaa Suci Sthana and drags one foot quickly and crosses it with the other.

Lankadahana : The dancer jumps up and comes down as in Ancita with this difference than she comes down obliquely and sits down after moving back.

Lankadahancita : The dancer moves round in Aflcits and sits down in Utkasasana, with her face towards the back of the stage.

Lasya : Delicate.

Lasyanga : A type of play.

Lata : The hands are extended obliquely at the sides.

Lataksepa : The dancer places one foot forward after placing it at her back and makes Nikutta on the ground.

Latakuncita : The left hand is in Lata while the right hand is arched. The hips move in Chinna. The legs are bent.

Latas : These having small fruits like grapes.

Latavetitaka : The hands are raised and moved in Udvestita towards the body and out to the sides. This is done obliquely and alternatey.

Latavrscika : One foot moves backward in Ancita with the toes curved up. The left hand is in Lata gestuse.

Laulya : Covetousness.

Lavani : The dancer stands in the Samapada Sthana and bends, her waist in Ardhacandra. Then she revolves her body, keeping her waist fixed.

Laya : A dance of fast tempo expressing astonishment.

Lehita : To lick the teeth or the lips.

Lekha : Letter.

Lekhana : Sarhyuta-hasta. The left hand in Pataka is raised while the right is placed on it in Sandamsa.

Lekhya Siddhi : Recording.

Lila : Sportive Mimicry.

Lilangahara : Sportive limbs.

Lina : The Pataka hands are replaced on the chest in Anjali. The neck is elongated while the shoulders are bent in Nihancita. The two pataka hands are held together in the Anjali position on the breast.

Lingastha : Observing vows.

Lohadi : The dancer stands in Sarna and turns round her hips. Then she jumps and comes down obliquely.

Lokadharmi : Popularly realistic representation. Realistic Practice.

Lola Movement : The eyes are moved.

Lolita : The dancer stamps the ground slowly and moves

without touching the ground. The hands are arched and moved in Recita. The head is moved in Lolita on all sides. The dancer stands in the Vaistlava Sthana.

Lopikas : Cakes.

Lopya : Worthy of omission.

Luthita : The dancer stands in Svastika and stamps the ground with the foreparts of her feet.

★★★★★

Mada : Inebriation.

Madalasa : The dancer places her feet unsteadily here and there as in intoxication.

Madanavati : The Atijagati Chandas of thirteen syllables if the first eight and the final.

Madaskhalitaka : The hands are let down, the head is in Parivahita and the feet are moved round and turned away in Aviddha Cari.

Madavilasita : The hands move in Dola and the feet in Svastikapasrta. Placing the hands in Anficita and Valita, the Talasarhghattiata Karana is performed. Nikuttaka, Urudvrtta, Karihasta and Katicchinna.

Madhukara Sadrsa : The first six syllables are short and the other long.

Madhukarika : The metre where the first two and the final one are long.

Madhuparka : Mixture of honey, curd, ghee, water and sugar.

Madhura Movement : A soothing glance.

Madhurya : Delicacy, Sweetness, Self-Possession.

Madhya : Medium.

Madhyacakra : The dancer stands after doing Nikunana. Then she again performs Nikuttana after turning round.

Madhyaluthlta : The dancer performs Nikutta and after a rest drags her feet and performs Nikutta.

Madhyama : Shaken finger. The dancer crosses her Pataka hands in Svastika and moves her head in Vidhuta. She stands in the Saiva Sthana and performs Katichinna with Hasya Drsti.

Madhyasta : Neutral, Non-committed.

Madhyasthapanakutta : Nikuttana is done in front and at the back. Then after placing them in the middle Nikuttana is again performed.

Madira Movement : There are three types of Taruna, Madhyama, Adhama, Inebriated.

Mahadevi : Empress.

Mahattara : Mationaly attendant.

Mahi Movement : A glance expressing greatness. The sixth and the eighth syllablesc are long.

Mainavi : The dancer moves her both sides. The dancer moves without rest like a fish in a well.

Makara : Alligator. The Pataka hands are placed on each other with the thumbs raised and curved.

Makaravartana : One hand in Makara is moved in Avartita to the front and at the sides.

Mala : Garland, Series of offers. Metre has sixteen syllables in every foot and all of them are long.

Malacindu : Cindu is done in an irregular series.

Malakara : Gardener.

Malina : Faded, Pallid.

Malina Movement : The eyelids flutter and the corners of the eyes are pale.

Mana : Jealous, Anger, Measure.

Manas : The wrist is bent outward.

Manavi : The dancer moves in circles and comes forwards repeatedly with her left hand placed on the hips and the right is in Khatakmunda.

Manda : Mild, The nostrils are drawn in or nostrils are at rest.

Mandala : Mystic diagrams, Circular places. The feet are placed obliquely four talas apart and they are turned sideways. The knees and the hips are kept normally.

Mandala Bharana : The hands describe a circle moving inward and then they are moved downard in Dola.

Mandalagra : One hand is moved while the other hand is raised. They are moved at the sides, to the front and at the back.

Mandala Svastika : The hands are placed in Svastika with the palms turned up and facing the front. The body should be in the Mandala Sthana.

Mandi : Dance of which the main feature is movements in a series.

Mandra : Grave accent, Low pitch movement.

Mandra Gati : Low pitch.

Manduki : The dancer walks almost like a lion with her hands in Sikhara.

Mani Bandhas : The movements of the wrist. One wrist rests on the other and they move in and out forming circles.

Mani Bandhasikarsa : The hands are raised to the shoulders and moved together or one after the other. The elbows are again moved outwards and inwards. Then they quickly describe a circle. They are rotated at the sides and then they are thrown outwards gracefully.

Manoratha : Indirect expression of desire, Mental wish.

Manthanrtya : The dancer dances once in Manthatala. Dhruvaka is done two to four times while Abhoga is done only once. Dhruva is again performed with various hand gestures.

Manthara : The eyes are opened.

Manusi : Human.

Manyu : Anger.

Marala : The dancer moves her heels and toes in Recita and stretches the feet forward.

Marana : Death.

Marda : Slackness.

Mardita Movements of Shanks : The sole of which the side is at an angle to the floor and rubs it.

Marga : Indication.

Marsaka : Worthy one.

Masmata : The dancer gestures with her hands and her eyes express Rasa through Snigdha Drsti.

Masrana Movement : A glance expresing love.

Mastaki : Forehead coronet.

Masuraka : Cushioned pillows.

Matalli : Make a whirling movement while throwing the two feet back, move hands on the Udvestiita and Apaviddha movements.

Mati : Self-assurance, Intellect, Discriminating judgement, Mind.

Matsya Karana : The dancer jumps and moves round her hips. Then she turns round with her left side like a fish.

Matsya Lolitaka : The dancer jumps as in Enapluta, moves her hips round and comes down to the ground obliquely.

Mattagati : Inebriated one.

Mattakrida : The dancer performs Bhramara and Nupura and then, with the right side of the body, she performs Bhujangat-rasita. He goes on to Vaisakharecita, Aksipta, Chinna, Bhramara, Vyarhsita, Uromandala, Nitamba, Karihasta and Katicchinna. The dancer revolves the back gracefully and, performs the Nupura Karanas. Bhujangatrasita should be performed with the left side of the body.

Mattalli : The left and the right feet are thrown back with a whirling movement. The hands move in Udvestita and thrown back.

Mattaskhalitaka : After the Mattalli Karana the right hand is moved round and bent to touch the Cheek. The dancer proceeds to Apaviddha quickly with Talasarhsphotita and finishes the Ailgahara by performing Karihasta and Katichinna.

Mattavarni : Side room.

Maulirecitaka : One hand rests on the hip and the other is stretched forward. Then they are moved upwards gracefully and brought to the ears.

Mavada : Do not speak.

Maya : Deceit.

Mayuralalita : Assume the Vrscika Karana, keep hands in Recita, turn the Trika (Sacrum) Vrscika is performed by one foot. The hands are moved in Recita. The hips are turned round.

Mayuri : The dancer moves her hands gradually upwards and slowly raises her feet. The dancer stands on her toes with her in Kapittha and shakes both her knees alternately.

Medha : Intellect, Intelligence.

Metre : Rhythm and Syllable of proper quality Aksara.

Misra : Mixed.

Mithahsamviksyabahya : One hand is moved straight up and placed on the shoulder on the other side.Then it is brought back to its own side and rotated.

Mithoyuta : Joined together.

Mleccha Gali : Barbarous tribes.

Mocaka : Ear pendants.

Moha : Fainting, Delusion or loss of sense.

Moksa : End, Releasing.

Moksa Kama : Desire for Salvation.

Moksana : Letting out, The motion of releasing.

Motana : Folding up, The motion of crushing.

Motita : One foot is in Sarna while the other is in Kuncita with the toes touching the ground. The hands are raised at the front in Karkata. The dancer jumps as in Kartari on both sides alternately. Her hands are in Tripataka.

Mottayita : Manifestation of affection.

Mrdava : Crushing contrasting.

Mrdu Angaharas : Gentle gesticulation and movements of the limbs.

Mrgasirsa : The thumb and the little finger are raised. The rest of the fingers are bent down together.

Mrgi : The dancer moves quickly to the front or sideways like a deer with her hands in Tripataka.

Mrt : Clay.

Mudita : Second, the third and the last two syllables are guru.

Mudra : Ring, The middle fingers and the thumbs are joined while the other fingers are extended.

Mudras : Hand gestures.

Mudupa : The dancer dance Mudupa Caris following the tala used in various gaits.

Mudupa Cari : Mucdupa is the upper side of a toe and the cari done with the Mudupa is called Mucdupa cari.

Mugdha Movement : A bright look.

Mukha : Opening, Beginning.

Mukha Raga : Facial colouring.

Mukha Vaivarnya : Pallor in the face, Mukhaja Facial.

Mukhanetraghurnana : Moving the face to face, rolling the eyes.

Mukharasa : While dancing the dancer utters words in order to express emotions.

Muktajala : Pearl-net.

Muktas : Free.

Muktavali : Pearl necklace.

Mukula : The fingers of the Harhsamukha hands are bent and close. The tips touch one another. Bud shaped.

Mukula Movement : The eyelashes flutter and their tips meet. The pupils meet in happiness.

Mukuta : Crown.

Munca : Leave off.

Mungarana : The dancer jumps from the Sarhhata position to the front and sits on the ground in Kukkutasana facing backwards.

Murajakartaricalaka : The hands are moved round from the chest to the shoulders. Then they are quickly brought from the chest to the sides. One hand is moved downwards while the other is moved round. Then they are placed on the hips facing each other and moved.

Murandari : The dancer performs Bhramari in between two Murandari.

Murcchanas : Modes.

Muru : The dancer repeatedly wrings and throws her body in Viksipta and Aksipta bringing forward her hands in Tripataka. The performance can also be done in the Aditala.

Murujadambara : The hands are moved round at the middle of the body, at the right and the left and at the sides. The right hand is raised to the left shoulder and quickly brought to the middle and then to the left while the other hand touches the navel.

Musti : Fist, The finger tips touch the palm and the thumb is placed on them.

Mustika Svastika : The Khatakamukha hands are bent at the wrists and moved round.

Mustivartana : The Musti hands are moved to the right and to the left in Vyavartana.

★★★★★

Nagabandha : Four talas, done at the same intervals, are performed separately. Each of them are divided into three and they are done separately. The hands and the feet are placed in their normal positions. The dancer moves round her head and places her fingers on her shoulders. The dancer sits and places her right shank on her left thigh.

Nadi : The first and the final syllables are long.

Nagapasarpita : Draw back feet from Svastika position Head in Parivahita and the hands in Recita.

Nagarakas : Citizens, Police constables.

Naiskramiki : Departing.

Naivedyas : Food offerings.

Nalika : Enigma.

Nalini : The Meter in which two Laghus and one Guru, The Fifth and the final syllables.

Nalinipadmakosa : The Padmakosa hands are moved in Vyavrtta and Parivartita.

Nama : Substantives, Name.

Namanika : The dancer bends her body easily and slowly adopting difficult postures.

Namavali : The dance is full of expressive actions.

Nandana : Joy giver.

Nandi : Benedictory utterances.

Nandi Padas : Sentences in the benedictory verse.

Nandyavarta : It is Vardhamana with the feet placed six or twelve angulas apart.

Narada : A quarrel monger.

Narma : Joke.

Narmadyuti : Flash of joke.

Narmagarbha : Covert pleasantry

Narman : Pleasanty.

Narmasphota : Unfoldment of pleasantry.

Narmasphurja : Sudden burt of pleasantry.

Nartaka : Dancer.

Nartaki : Danseuse.

Nartanabharana : Bahyabhramari, Nihsanka, Hormayi and Dantu are performed consecutively.

Nasakapolaspandana : Throbbing of the nose and the check.

Nasya and **Bastividhi :** Sternutatory and diulectic.

Nata : Bent, The nostrils are repeatedly contracted. Where the Face is bent down.

Nata Movement : To bend slightly one hip and its corresponding side and to move the shoulder away a little.

Nata Movement of Knee : To kneel to the ground.

Nata Movements of Shanks : The knees are bent so that the shanks may be bent.

Natajanuka : The dancer moves on her heels.

Nataka : Drama.

Natakiya : Actress.

Nataprstha : The dancer performs Kapalacurnana and raises her breast doing Calasana.

Nataraja : King of Dancers.

Natha : Lord.

Natra : The dancer moves in the Marala gati.

Natya Dharmi : Conventional Practice. Theatrically conventional

Natya Samgraha : Collection of component items in a dramatic performance.

Nirupana : Review of fulfillment and Succes in aramatic performance.

Natya Yoga : Activity of dance.

Natyacarya : Preceptor.

Natya Dharma : Conventional practice.

Natyagrha : Stage.

Natyakara : Play-wright.

Natyapravrttis : Usage in local vogue.

Natyasya Matrasca : The mothers presiding over the dramatic performance.

Natyopakaranas : Accessories to the dramatic production.

Navaratna Mukha : The hands are moved in Calakas such as Vislistavartita and then while doing a Vartana raised up to the hair, forming a Svastika. The palms are turned down. The hands are then rotated in Aviddha and Apaviddha together or alternately with a swinging movement.

Navata : Newness of acquaintance.

Naya : Good tactics.

Nayakas : Heroes.

Nayanacalana : Movements of the eyes.

Nayikas : Heroines.

Nepathya : Green room, Costumes and make up room.

Nepathyaja : Provoked by the costume.

Nepathyaja Hasya : Provoked by the costume and make up.

Neri : The dancer stands in the Caturasra Sthana and moves her foot in the Rathacakra Gati. The rhythm is Rasatala and the tempo is slow. The dancer moves her Pataka hand in all directions simulating the movement of a swinging cord. The dancer moves her limbs harmoniously and Sausthava is observed.

Nibhrta : Sober.

Nibhrta Movement : The eyes are cast down.

Nica : Low pitch, Inferior.

Nicapatra Gati : Lowly persons.

Nidarsana : Unfavourable precedent.

Nidra : Sleep, Drowsiness, Slumber.

Nigraha : Killing or curbing, Arrest. To lower.

Nigrantha : To Lower.

Nigrhita : Controlled, Arrested.

Nihancita Movement : The nostrils are expanded and the eyes are raised. The shoulder is raised and the neck is bent down.

Nihsanka : The dancer performs Sulu, joins her feet, jumps up and lands at some distance.

Nihsrta Movements of Shanks : The shanks assume this position upon moving the knees forward.

Nija Movements of Shanks : The toes touch the ground and the feet are motionless.

Nijapana : This is distinguished by Sausthava and Rekha and Gati and is full of beautiful Bhavas. The dancer looks at her hands.

Nikuficaka : The thumb of the Pataka hand touches the base of the middle finger.

Nikunca : The wrist is bent outward.

Nikuncita : Feet to be moved as in the Vrscika Karana and both hands bent at the sides, right hand held at the tip of the nose. barely touching it.

Nikuttaka : The dancer stands on bent toes. The hands move in Nikuttaka between the head and the arm. The feet are also moved in Nikutta. The right hand assuming Caturasra, is moved in Aviddhavakravartana and the right foot is moved in Udghattita. This action is, repeated by the left hand and the left foot.

Nila : Blue.

Nilatoya : The metre that has the second syllable Laghu and all the others long.

Nimeqa : To close the eyelids.

Nimesa : Closing.

Ninda : Censure.

Nipata : Particle.

Nipidita : Pressed.

Nirajita : The hands are crossed in Svastika and then separated by moving them outwards. They are obliquely moved round together near the head at the right and the left sides.

Nirakanksa : Devoid of expectation.

Nirbhugna : Not bent, Raised up. The chest is steady and the back is curved. The shoulder is raised. The face is lowered.

Nirdesa : Suggestion, Command direction.

Nirghata : Thunder storm, Earthquake.

Nirlajja : Impendent.

Nirnaya : Ascertainment.

Nirodha : Hindrance.

Nirukta : Convincing explanation; Etymology.

Nirvahana : Conclusion.

Nirveda : Despondency, Dejectedness and indifference to worldly joys.

Niryhas : Type of ornamental figurine.

Nisada : Right hand-Index finger. The dancer moves her hands in Karihasta and glancing charmingly she moves her head in Vidhuta.

Niskramah : Going out. Projecting forward.

Nissabda : Silent.

Nistambhita : One foot in Kuncita, is moved back. The chest is in Samunnata. The hand is placed in Tilaka.

Nisthi Vana : Spitting.

Nisthura : Cruel.

Nitamba : Arms at the outset are thrown up with fingers pointing upwards. The arms are raised with the palms facing each other. Then the Baddha Cari is performed. The feet cross in Svastika. The Pataka hands, with the fingers pointing down are brought near the head and moved out from the shoulder in Parivrtta. They are placed in the Nitambavartana.

Nitambas Vastika : The hands are bent and placed on the hips. The feet are moved away from Svastika. The right side is bent.

Nitambavartana : The hands assume Nitamba from Alapallava and move down from the shoulders and brought near the hips.

Nithura Movement : The pupils are hidden under the eye lids.

Nivartanam : Turning sideways.

Nivartita : To look round.

Nivedana : Making it known.

Nivesa : Both the hands kept on the chest that is in Nirbhugna state. The dancer assumes the Mandala Sthana.

Nivi : Land of the clothes over the waist.

Nivrtta : Face turned towards the front, Hands and feet thrown out. Turned up.

Nivrtta Movement : To turn the hips to face the audience.

Nivrttavira Rasa : Excludes Vira Rasa.

Niyata phalaprtipti : Certainty of attainment.

Niyuddha : Wrestling.

Nrpa : King.

Nrtta : Dance.

Nupura : The hips should be turned round gracefully. The hands should move in Lata and Recita. One foot should perform Nupura. The lower spine gracefully turned round Bhramari Cari, Pada Cari.

Nupurapadika : The dancer moves one Ancita foot backwards. Then she quickly touches the ground with her toes.

Nupuraviddhika : The dancer stands with her legs crossed in Svastika and then performs Recita with her heels and toes.

Nyanavistara : Gaping of the eyes.

Nyasa and **Apanyasa :** Terminal and Semi terminal note.

Nyaya Dapetam : Logical defect.

★★★★★

Oh : He.

Ojas : Grandeur, Strength.

Osthadamsana : Biting the lips.

Osthya : Lebrals.

★★★★★

Pada : Foot, Music.

Padadvayanikutta : Nikuttana is done with both feet.

Padakranta : One foot is curved and pointed upward. The other foot is placed forward. The hands are raised in Dola.

Padapaviddhaka : The Khatakamukha hands are placed on the navel with palms turned upwards. The feet are in Sucividdha and Apakranta.

Padarecaka : The dancer moves her feet in various ways from one side to another. The heels and the toes are repeatedly moved inwards and outwards. They are raised and curved.

Padarthas : Objects.

Padasaukumarya : Delicacy of words, Agreeableness.

Padasthitinikuttita : The dancer stands on the toes with one foot in Nikuttana. This is repeated several times.

Padma : Lotus.

Padma Bandha : Four talas are followed as in Ravicakra. The hands and the feet meet each other, separately. It is performed to the Vasutala.

Padma Kosa : All the fingers, including the thumb, are bent, keeping them separated from each other without the tips touching.

Padmavartana : The hands are moved gracefully.

Padoccaya : Multiplex predication.

Paksapradyotaka : The hands are upturned in opposite directions. and placed on the waist. The Tripataka hands are placed on the top of the hips.

Paksisardulaka : The dancer moves round with her hands standing in Mandala.

Pallava : The Pataka hands are slackened at the wrists.

Pancama : Right hand ring finger. The dancer moves her hand in Alapallava while her head moves in huta.

Pandu : Yellowish white.

Paniprahatas : Hand strokes.

Pankti : The first three and the last one.

Pannagas : Serpents

Parakrama : Valour.

Parastha : Another person, Extraneous.

Parasvaga : Palm kept obliquely.

Paravrtta : The big toe and the little toes are kept at the same level as the heel. The dancer performs the Janita Kara first and then stretching out one foot, proceeds to the Alataka Karanas and revolves the back. The left hand is bent and touches the cheek. The Angahara is finished by performing Katichinna. The Janita Karanas is performed on the right side of the body. Then after performing the Sakatasya Kara and the Alataka Karanas, Bhramara is performed on the left. With hands moving in Nikuna, the dancer performs Karihasta and finishes the Ailgahara by performing the Katichinna Karala.

Paribhasana : Accusation.

Paribhvand : Surprise.

Parichinna : The feet are placed together and the dancer performs Parichinna, followed by Apaviddha or, the Sambhranta Karanas. Then the dancer performs Bahyabhra-maraka, proceeding to Vamasuci.

Parictirika : Chaperon.

Parigraha : Acceptance, To end fold.

Parikara : Enlargement, Establishment.

Parimarjana : Ritualistic cleaning.

Pariparsvika : Assistant.

Paripdati : Specified days by turns.

Parisarpa : Pursuit.

Parivartaka : Change of action.

Parivartana Nandi : Benediction .

Parivartanas : Walking round.

Parivartita Karana : The fingers, beginning from the little finger are moved outward.

Parivartita Movements of Shanks : The shank's are moved back from the position in which they had been. The knees touch the ground with the shanks behind them.

Parivrajakas : Way faring sages.

Parivrtta : The hands are raised in Apavestita, the feet are moved round in Suci. The hips are turned round. The dancer moves round in the Bhramari Cari.

Parivrttakarecita : Placing the Svastika and Vipraklrna hands over the head the dancer bends the body and moves the left hand in Recita. The body is raised and the Recita hand is repeated. Vrscika with the Lata hand is performed, followed by Recita.

Paroksa : Invisible.

Parsniga Movements of Shanks : To move backwards on the heels.

Parsniparspagata : One heel is placed on the inner side of the other.

Parsnisanghatita : The hands in Kartarimukha are arched over the chest. The heels rub against the thighs.

Parsnividdha : The heel touches the big toe.

Parsvaccheda : The dancer moves the hands in Nikutta on the chest, and performs Ordhvajanu.

Parsvadvaya Cari : The dancer stands on the toes and performs Nikurtana followed by Svastika from which she moves her feet to Nikuttana first at one side and then at the other.

Parsvaga Movements of Shanks : The dancer moves her feet sideways or stands at the side of the stage.

Parsvagata : Side head gear.

Parsvagrahana : Holding the sides.

Parsvajanu : One foot in Sarna position and the opposite thigh is lifted up. One foot is kept normally and the other is placed on the thigh. One hand is placed in Musti on the chest.

Parsvakranta : One foot in Kuncita is raised and the knee is brought up to the level of the breast. Finally, the foot is moved in Udghattita. The foot is put forward after doing Apakranta. The hands are moved in harmony.

Parsva Mandala : The hands are moved in circles at the sides.

Parsvanikuttaka : Svastika hands to be held on one side the feet Nikuttita. The hands are in Svastika and they any placed on one side. The feet are in Nikuna. The left foot is slightly bent and the right foot moves in Nikuna. The face rests on the left shoulder.

Parsvapani : Side handed.

Parsva Suci : The dancer stands on her toes and touches the ground on one side with one knee.

Parsvasvastika : Svastika and then Nikuttaka are performed.

The hand is turned over and placed on the thigh. The Parsvasvastika Angahara is finished by performing Urudvrtta, Aksipta, Nitamba, Karihasta and Katicchinna successively.

Parvans : Sections.

Paryastaka : The dancer performs Talapuspaputa, Apaviddha, Varitita. The Angahara is continued by performing the Nikugaka, or Udvrtta, Aksipta, Uromandala, Nitamba, Karihasta, and Katicchinna Karanas successively.

Paryayagajadanta : One hand is moved obliquely while the other hand is stretched alternately.

Paryupasana : Pacification.

Pasa : Noose, Pascat.

Purahsara : The same is done first at the back then in front (i.e. in reverse).

Pasupaksi Gati : Animals and Birds movement.

Patah : Letting it down relaxation.

Pataka : Episode. The thumb is bent to touch the root of the forefinger and the rest of the fingers are kept close together and extended.

Patakasthana : Episode Indication.

Patakasvastika : The hands cross in Pataka with one palm turned up and the other turned down.

Patakavartana : The wrists are moved to the right and left in Pataka.

Patana : Letting down. To look downwarcds. To lower the eyebrows together or one after the other.

Patava : The dancer stamps on the ground with one foot.

Pathika Gati : Wayfarer.

Pathya : Recitation, Passage for declamation.

Patita : Fallen.

Patitotpatita : The right leg is bent and one foot is moved up and downs. The hands follow the movements of the foot.

Pauskara : Instruments Drums etc.

Payasa : Milk pudding.

Perani : The dancer decorates her body with Bhasma and dances with Ghargharika moving rhythmically.

Phaivata : The dancer moves her hands in Kangula, looks with Blbhatsa Drsti, moves her head in Paravrtta and stands in the Pratyalidha Sthana.

Phalartha : Sake of fruit i.e. progeny.

Phalayoga : Attainment of the fruit.

Phena : Froth from mouth.

Phulla : Blown up. The cheeks are blown out.

Pidibata : The dancer stamps the ground alternately with the sole of one or both foot.

Pihita : Concealed. To keep the eyelids still.

Pindi Bandhas : Group dances

Pisacas : Vampires

Pistalmtta : The right foot performs Suci while the left foot performs Apakranta. Then both the feet perform Bhujangatrasita. The dancer moves round in Bhujangatrasita.

Pita : Yellow.

Pitamaha : Brahma.

Pitrs : Manes.

Pitta : Bile Possibility of attainment.

Prarambha : Beginning.

Prabhava : Mighty influence.

Prabhavati : Metre in which the fourth and sixth syllables constitute.

Prabodha : Waking up, Pracchannakamita, Concealment of love.

Praddna : Making gifts.

Pradesni : The index finger.

Pradvivakas : Judicial officers.

Pragalbhya : Courage, Maturity.

Pragamana : Moving forward.

Prahdras : Strokes.

Prakampita : Quivering. The chest incessantly heaves up and down.

Prakara : Variety, Aspect.

Prakarana : Contexts, Prakasanam.

Prakasita : Fourth the sixth and the final syllables are long.

Prakasyanam : Disclosing things to be disclosed.

Praklta : The pupils are kept normally.

Prakrta : The rustic and unrefined. Episodical incident.

Prakrta Pathya : Characteristics of Prakritaric recitation, Laksana.

Prakrtam : Natural or usual position.

Prakrti : Role, Characters, Basis.

Praksepya : Worn over.

Pralambita : Suspended down.

Pralapa : Prattling.

Pralaya : Loss of Sense, Sinking, Fainting.

Pralokita : Careful observance. To look sideways.

Pramana Kala : Normal kala.

Pramanas : Authorities.

Pramoda : Joy.

Prapanca : Compliment.

Prapanika : Trader.

Prapti : Discovery, Attainment, Accession.

Praptisambhava : To stretch the eyelids.

Prarocana : Foresight, Laudation.

Prarthana : Supplication.

Prasa : Spike.

Prasada : Perspicuity.

Prasadiki : Calming. Pleasing.

Prasamana : Calming, Subduing.

Prasamsa : Praise.

Prasanga : Reverence.

Prasangika : Subsidiary.

Prasanna Movement : A pleasing glance with smiling eyes.

Prasara : The dancer moves her Aviddhavakra hands and performs the Parsnirecitika Cari with other appropriate for the performance. It is done in a slow tempo and to a rhythm of one beat.

Prasarita : Extended.

Prasarita Movement : The sides are stretched. The arm is extended to the front. The toes are straight and motionless.

Prasarpitaka : One hand in Recita and the other with Lata gesture. The feet are dragged on the ground and rubbing it.

Prasasti : Benediction.

Prasava : Confinement of the queen.

Prasiddhi : Celebrity.

Prasnikas : Arbitrators, Assessors, Judges.

Prasnna : Pleased.

Prasrta : Spread out.

Prastavana : Prologue.

Pratapa : Aggressiveness.

Pratayayas : Suffixes.

Prathita : Well established.

Pratihari : Portress.

Pratiksepas : Laudatory songs.

Pratilomanulomaka : The order of Anuloma Viloma is exactly reversed.

Pratimukha : Progression.

Pratipaksa : Bhyasuyikas, Unable to brook rivals.

Prativartana : The Alapallava hands are thrown backward and rotated

Pratyaksa : Visible.

Pratyalidha : The Aliciha Sthana is reversed by extending the left foot and bending the right.

Pratyutpannamatitva : Presence of Mind.

Pravesa : Entry, Entrance.

Pravesaka : Introductory scene.

Pravesrsana : To draw in the pupils.

Pravespitakaracarana : Trembling of the hands and feet.

Pravrddhaka : Too advanced in age.

Pravrddhanada : Swelling uproar.

Pravri : Rainy season.

Pravrta : The dancer turns round herself delicately with her foot in Udvrtta.

Pravrttaka : Personal Business.

Pravrtti : Action, To move onwards, Local Usages.

Prayalidha : The Alidha Mandala is reversed.

Prayatna : Effort.

Prayayi Movement : A pleasing glance.

Prayoga : Performance.

Prayoga Sauksmya : Delicacy of its production.

Prayogaprada : Sarhyutahasta. The Pataka hands are joined at their tips.

Prayogatisaya : Particular presentation.

Prccha : Interrogation.

Preksa : Dramatic performance.

Preksakanam : Spectators.

Premagarbhi Movement : A pleasing glance.

Prenkhana : The dancer places one foot by the side of the heel of the other. Her hands are in Kurma.

Prenkhola Movement : The eyes look at an object and then are drawn away from it.

Prenkholitaka : After observing the Dola Pada Cari.

Prerita : The dancer stamps on the ground at her side with one foot placed at a distnace of twenty-seven inches from the other. Then she stands with her knees slightly and obliquely bent. One of her hands is placed on the chest in Sikhara while the other hand is extended in Pataka.

Presanacarika : Maid for running errands.

Pretikholita : The dancer moves her body in half circles, first backward and then forward. The hands are contracted at the end.

Priya : Dear.

Priyam Vacanam : Compliment.

Priyokti : Pleasing utterance compliment.

Pronnata : The toes are kept at the same level with the instep. The body is in Ayata.

Prsthaluthita : The feet are in Kuncita while the toes are moved to the back. Then they are moved to the original position in front.

Prsthanusari : The arms moves to the back.

Prsthasvastika : The hands move in Viksiptaksipta. The feet cross each other in Svastika. Apakranta and Ardha Suci are performed. The arms are extended in UdveHita.

Prsthotksepa : The dancer performs Utksepa only at her back.

Prsthottanatala : One foot is moved back touching the ground with the back of the toes.

Pulaka : Hairs standing on ends.

Pupaputa : The Sarpasirsa hands, with their fingers close to one another, meet on one side closely.

Purah Pascatsara : Nikuttana is done in front of the body and at the back. Then with the back of the toes.

Purahkesepanikuttita : Nikuttana is done in front on the back of the toes. After resting the feet for a while Nikuttana is done again.

Purahksepa : The dancer throws up her Kuncita foot and stretches it forward quickly. Then she places it on the ground.

Purastatluthita : The feet are dragged to the front.

Purna : Full or Heptatonic. To blow the cheeks enough to make them founded.

Purna Movement : To distend the belly.

Purodandabhramya : One hand in Musti is obliquely moved in and out while the other hand is moved gracefully. The hands are alternately stretched forward.

Purvam : Outset.

Purvaranga : Preliminary item.

Purvavakya : Retrospect.

Puskara Dosa : Defects in the playing of the drum.

Puspa : Sweet words.

Puspaputavartana : One hand in Puspaputa is moved in Parivartana and then placed on the chest after moving it in Vyavartana.

Pusta : Model work.

Putraka : Son.

★★★★★

Racita : The neck is shaken and moved sideways.

Ragaprptih : Accession to feeling in production Prayogasyam.

Raja : King.

Rajaka : Washerman, Dyer.

Rajasevaka : King's officer.

Rajasyala : Brother of the chief mistress of the king.

Rajnajala : Jewel.

Rajopacara : Royal etiquette.

Raksa : To protect.

Rakta : A reddened face. Endearing, Red.

Raktam : Pleasing.

Ramya : The Fourth syllables are Guru in the metre.

Rangapitha : Stage.

Rangasirasa : Stage head.

Rasa : Sentiment.

Rasa and **Gandha :** Taste and odour.

Rasa Paka : Ripeness of Rasa.

Rasadrstis : Glances expressing, Sentiments.

Rasmi : Reins rays.

Rathacakra : The dancer stands in the Caturasra Sthana and slides her feet forward and backward touching the ground.

Rathanetni : The hands in Rathacakra are crossed in Svastika and held obliquely.

Rati : Love.

Ratibhava : Emotional fervour of love.

Ratnamalika : Jewel string.

Rattamuru : The dancer twist her body repeatedly and violently.

Raudra : Furious sentiments, Impetuous anger, Terrible.

Raudra Rasa : Impetuous anger of wrath.

Raudri : In the form of the trident.

Raudri Movement : The eyes are open, bloodshot and still.

Ravicakra : The dancer dances to six even measured talas. Each tala is done twice to form one unit and the units are performed one after another to accompany six Sthanas. These twelve talas are done as in Cakrabandha.

Ravisacara : The dancer performs Bahyabhramari Dantu, Hormayi and Nihsanka consecutively.

Rayadi Paksisalava : Nihsanka and Dandu are performed in the air.

Rayarailgalu : The dancer throws upward one of her feet in Sulu and repeats the same with the other.

Recaka : Hand. Circular motion of the neck. Loosening, Moved about. The feet move in Nikuncita while the hands are in Recita. The hips are also moved in Recita.

Recita : The hands in Harpsapakssa are moved quickly with their palms turned up. The hands move in Recita, the dancer bends sideways and again moves the hands in Recita. To raise one eyebrow.

Recita Movement : To move the hips in all directions.

Recita Movements of Shanks : The dancer moves on her toes raising her heels. The feet must be at an angle to the ground.

Recitanikugita : The hands move in Recita. The right foot moves in Nikutta. The left hand moves in Dola.

Recitanikuttita : Right hand. Recita, left foot. Udghattita, left hand. Dola gesture.

Recitavartana : The hands are separated from Svastika and quickly moved round forming Recita.

Repugnant : Undesirable.

Riktapurnaa Movement : The belly is first down in, than distended.

Rim : Flat lip.

Romasa : Hairy, Bushy.

Romlineca : Horripilation.

Rsabha : Left Middle ring finger. The right hand in Hamsasya and the left hand in Ardhacandra, are placed on the hips. The head is kept straight and the dancer stands in the Brahma Sthana.

Rtus : Seasons.

Rucika : Bracelet.

Ruksa Movement : A dull and colourles look.

Rupa : Beauty. Supposition, Form.

Rupaka : Metaphor.

Rupakas : Dramas.

Rupanusarini : Close by emulative.

★★★★★

Samslesa : Joining together.

Sabda : Word, Sound.

Sabdacali : Sthanaka, Cari, Khanda, Mandala and Karanas are performed with appropriate Hastas. Pramana is observed.

Sabdavan : Audible.

Sabdhacyuta : Lapse in a Word-slang.

Saci : A Kuncita foot raised and placed ahead on the ground, Two hands in harmony with the perfonnance. Askance.

Sadavakrta : Hexatonic.

Saddharanas : Overlapping, Common to two.

Sadga: The right hand is moved ih Alapadma and the left hand in Catura. The dancer moves round in Mayuralalita and Sadga.

Sadharana : The hands rest on the hips and then they are obliquely moved. They describe a circle together moving inward and outward.

Sadja : Left hand ring finger.

Sadrsi : Similarity, Uniqueness.

Sagarva : The eyes are raised with pupils still.

Saghosa Kataka : Sounding Kataka Sahaja Natural.

Sahaja : To keep the eyebrows normally.

Sahaja Movement : To place the belly naturally.

Saharsa : The eyes look as if they want to speak.

Saiva : The left foot is in Sarna while the other is raised to the level of the knee-cap (of the other foot) in Kuncita.

Sakamksa : Full of expectation.

Sakara Gati : King's brother-in-law.

Sakatasya : The body is at rest. One foot is stretched in Talasaficara and the chest is in Udvahita. The body is straight, one foot is put forward in Agratalasancara. The right foot performs Janita first and goes on to Nikuttaka and Sakatasya while the left foot performs Askandita. The dancer moves round with her feet in Sakatasya.

Sakra : Indra.

Saktasya : At the outset the body is in rest. Then advance with a Talasancara foot keep the chest in Udvahita.

Sakti : Power, Placation.

Sakuta Movement : A glance full of meaning.

Sakvar : Fourteen syllables.

Salabhanjikas : Figurines.

Salailganeri : The Neri is performed with single and double hand gestures.

Sallapaka : Harsh discourse.

Sama Movement : To keep the hips and neck in a natural position. The eyes are charming and serene. The head is kept straight and motionless in a natural way. The natural position of the chest. To keep the eyelids normally.

Samadhi : Concentrations.

Samakartarilohadi : The feets are crossed in Svastika at the beginning and at the end of the performance.

Samakartaryancita : The dancer stands in Sarna and then crosses her Aflcita feet in Svastika.

Samam : Level, Harmoniouss.

Samanakha : The dancer stands in Sarna and exends her feet obliquley. The feet are joined in Samanakha. The hands are let down while the body is kept normally. The two feet touch each other with the nails symmetrical, Two hands hanging down.

Samanas : Similar features.

Samanmatha Movement : An excited glance.

Samanya Abhinaya : Basic Representation.

Samanya Gunas : Common qualities.

Smaya Samapada : The body is kept normally while the feet are straight and placed twelve angulas apart.

Samapada : The dancer stands with her feet together in Samanskha. The feet are in Sarna and placed one tala apart. Sausthava is observed.

Samapadancita : The dancer stands in Sarna and performs Ancita. Then she touches the ground with one shoulder and turns round sideways waving her feet.

Samapadanikuttita : Nikuttana is done with same feet on the toes.

Samapani : Level handed.

Samaprakosthavalana : The fore arms are rotated.

Samasa : Compounds.

Samaskhalitika : The dancer stamps with her feet obliquely and simultaneously forward and backward.

Sama Suci : The dancer touches the ground with her toes and knees. The heels, the shanks and the things touch the ground and the legs are extended obliquely.

Samata : Smoothness.

Samatva : Co-ordination.

Samavayaja : Growing out of the combination.

Samaya : Deliverance.

Sambhoga : Love in union, Sexual dalliance.

Sambhranta : One hand in the Vyavartita movement is kept on the thigh in Aviddha. One hand is moved in Avartita and it is then arched over the thigh. The dancer performs Ardha Suci, and then Dandapad on the left.

Sambrama : Excitement. The palm of the Arala hand is slightly hollowed and the forefinger touches the thumb.

Samdna Sabda : The same set of words.

Samghata: Breach of Alliance.

Samgraha : Synopticgist, Propitiation, Concealment.

Samhata : The body is kept normaly. The soles are joined together and so are the ankles.

Samhata Movement of Knee : The knees touch each other.

Samkananeri : The dancer performs the Neri with her hands moved in Nrttahasta gestures, done with one or both the hands.

Samksepa : Concealment,Taking away.

Samksiptaka : Compression.

Samksobha : Commotion.

Samlagna : The toes are joined together.

Samlapa : Dialogue.

Samlidhdna : Settling.

Sammoha : Fainting.

Samotsarita : The dancer extends her hands with her palms turned upwards and moves them continuously in Udvestita and Avestita. She places her left hand on her hips and moves round her right hand in Avartita. She moves round doing the Cari.

Samotsaritamattali : The dancer goes backward in a circular movement with her feet.

Sampat : Couplet.

Sampheta : Conflict. Mutual conflict, Angry words.

Sampraddna : Handing over, Sampradluirana, Elaborate thinking.

Sampravesanam : Withdrawal, Drawing within.

Samsaya : Hesitation and doubt Samyutakarana with both the hands joined.

Sandastaka : Biting.

Samskara : Consecration of words i.e. Grammar.

Samskrta : The Urban, the polished and civilized.

Samslesa : To join.

Samudgaka : Closed up like a chest.

Samudgaka : Pouting with the lower lip.

Samudvrtta : To raise the pupils.

Samudvrttah : Raising up.

Samunnata Movement : The hip, the arm and the shoulder. Lifted up.

Samvaddi : Consonant.

Samvarana : Concealment.

Samyas : Conformities.

Samyuta : Combined, Joined together.

Sancari : Bhava, Drstis, Glances regarding Transitory States.

Sancarika : The dancer bends one foot, throws it up repeatedly and brings it down obliquely to touch the other.

Sandasta : Bitten. The lower lip is pressed by the teeth.

Sandesa : Massages

Sandhi : Phonetic, Change, Junction.

Sandhima : Joined objects, Joints.

Sandhyanga : Limbs.

Sandolita : The dancer swings her Kuncita foot at her back.

Sanecari : Moving or Transitory.

Sanghataja : Growing out of contrast.

Sanghattita : The dancer stands in the Visama Suci Sthana, jumps up and when she comes down she stamps on the ground with her feet.

Sanghatya : Grouped together.

Sanjiva : Living creatures.

Sanka : Apprehension. Suspicious. The dancer quickly whirls round and moves her body towards the front and the sides.

Sankirna : Mixed.

Sankita : Fearfully uneasy, Apprehensive.

Sankita Movement : The glance is sometimes steady and sometimes still. The eyes are sightly raised, obliquely open and the pupils are unsettled.

Sanmukhinarathanga : The Recita hands are obliquely moved facing each other. They are moved inwards at the sides with their elbows pointing.

Sannata : Gesture with both the hands. Leap forward, then place the feet forward in Svastika form.

Santa Movement : The eyes are steady and they look downwards.

Saptadvipas : Seven great divisions of the world.

Saptasvaras : Full.

Sarana : One foot is brought down to the ground with the heel of the other foot. The hands assume Pataka.

Sarasama : Conforming in syllables.

Sarasandhana : One hand is moved to the back while the other hand is repeatedly raised to the head.

Sarasas : Cranes Pluta.

Sarasvati : Goddess of speech.

Sarika : The dancer glides one foot forward.

Sarimata : The dancer jumps up and places her feet forward in Svastisa. The hands are bent.

Sarira : Corporeal, Bodily.

Sarira Abhinaya : Histrionic, Representation through physical-limbs.

Sarna : The cheeks keep naturally. To keep the wrist straight.

Sarna Movement of Knee : The knees are kept normally.

Sarna Movements of Shanks : The dancer rests her feet in a natural position.

Sarpa : Serpents.

Sarpagati : Serpentine movements.

Sarpasirsa : All the fingers, including the thumb, are close to one another and the palm is hollowed.

Sarpita : Both the feet to be moved from Ancita position, head is in Parivahita gesture, hands in Recita.

Sarupya : Identity.

Sarvagata : Total.

Sarvangahara : Cold.

Sasambhrama : The eyes are agitated.

Sasita : Squeezing up all the limbs.

Sasprha Movement : A glance expressing desire.

Sastra : Treatise.

Sataghni : Hundred -killer.

Satha : Deceitful.

Sathbhranta : The dancer performs the Viksipta Karana, moving the hands and the feet in accordance with the expression of the face. Suci is performed on the left side of the body and the left hand is thrown outwards while the right hand rests on the chest. The back is revolved. Then Nupura, Aksiptaka, Ardhasvastika, Nitamba, Karihasta, Uromandala and Katichinna should be performed successively by the dancer to end the Sathbhranta Karanas.

Sattva : Latent strength, Temperament.

Sattva Darsana : Sight of Apparitions.

Sattvaja : Originating.

Sattvati : Grand Conception of the mind.

Sauksmya : Fineness.

Saumya : Gentle one from the mind, Temperamental.

Saurya : Heroism.

Sausthava : Perfection.

Savipralambha : Pleasantry in regard to love in.

Savyagra : An eager look.

Savyatha : A painful glance.

Sayanavastha : Lying down posture.

Sddhu : Well-done.

Sddhuvdda : Uttering words of congratulation.

Sddhya : Yet to be derived.

Sdhasa : Rashness.

Sentiment : Rasa.

Sici : To look obliquely and to cover the eyes with the lashes.

Siddhi : Successful achievement. Persuasion.

Sikha : Tuft of hair.

Sikhara : Summit. The thumb of the Musti hand is raised.

Sikhi : Peacock.

Silpakarini : Crafts woman.

Silpi : Expert in fine arts.

Siluka : The dancer moves her Harhsapaksa hands and performs Kullrika and one other similar to it on all sides and moves forward. She moves the sole of one foot in Vanarakridita.

Simhakarsita : One foot stretched backwards, hands to be bent and turned round in the front.

Simhapluta : Tirapabhramari, Rayarailgalu, Dantu and Hormayi are performed consecutively.

Simhavikridita : The dancer performed Alata and moves quickly. The hands are moved in harmony.

Simhi : The dance stands on her toes and jumps quickly to the front. Her hands are in Sikhara.

Siras : Head.

Sirihira : The dancer places one foot in Sarna, puts the other forward and shakes her shank.

Siripidi : The dancer repeatedly moves forward and backward touching the ground with her soles.

Siro Bhramari : The dancer stands on her hand, raises her feet and turns round thrice.

Sirsa Jala : Hair net.

Sirsanuvalita : The hands in Mustika Svastika are moved above the head.

Sirsavalita : The right foot and the head are moved round in backwards. The hands are bent and ther move Up and down.

Sisya Nispadana : Ability to impart to the disciple.

Sita : White.

Sitkara : Hissing sound, One shivers etc.

Skandha Bhanga : Acute pain in the shoulders as though they are broken.

Skandha Bhranta : The dancer assumes Utkatasana and performs Ancita. She touches the ground with her shoulders, lifts her feet in the air and then touching the ground with her hands turns round as in Bhrantapadancita. Finally, she stands facing four directions successively.

Skandhanata : The head is bent towards the shoulder.

Skandhancita : The dancer performs Ancita and touches the ground with her shoulders. Then she jumps obliquely and quickly comes down.

Skhalita : The dancer performs Dolapada and moves her hands round in harmony. The dancer moves her feet in round and places them on the ground. Her hands are contracted and bent. Her face is brought slightly forward.

Slagha : Willingness to serve and gain praise.

Slesa : Union, Combination, Synthesis.

Slittvika : Temperamental.

Smera Movement : The eyebrows, eyelids and pupils are quivering.

Smita : Gentle smile.

Smrti : Recolleetion, Memory.

Snigdha : Loving. glance.

Snigdha Movement : A graceful look. The eyes are pleasing and slightly open.

Snigdhatva : Smoothness.

Sobha : Beauty, Brilliance, Brilliant character.

Socchvasa : Having the respiration. The air is drawn in.

Soka : Sorrow, Grief.

Sokdvastha : Sorrowful mood.

Sopalambha : Full of words of rebuke and taunt karananuv iddha.

Soprasa Movement : An anxious look.

Sotka Movement : A distant glance expressing love.

Sotsuka Movement : To look back again and again.

Spandita : One foot is put forward five talas apart from the other.

Sparsa : Touch.

Sphita Movement: The eyebrows, eyelashes and pupils are shining.

Sphotana : Bursting. To disengage.

Sphurika : The dancer glides forward with both feet, placed in the Sarna Sthana.

Sphurita : The dancer quickly moves her feet forward touching the ground with their sides. To tremble the eyelids.

Sphuta : Distinct.

Sraddha : Faith.

Srama : Exhaustion, Weariness.

Sranta : Tired, Exhausted.

Sranta Movement : The eyelids droop due to fatigue, the corners of the eyes are contracted and the pupils are lowered. The eyelids are raised and move slothfully. The eyes are fixed on a nearby object.

Srngara : Erotic. Lives. Love.

Srngaravan : Don Juan.

Srngarinigati : Gait in the sentiment of love.

Srotogata : Flowing like a current.

Sruva : The dancer moves her body like a flame in a breeze.

Stabadha : Puffed up, Stubborn.

Stabdha Movement : The eyes are still.

Stambha : Paralysis.

Stambhakridanika : The dancer extends one of her feet obliquely and touches its side with the sole of the other foot repeatedly.

Stambhana : Rigidity. The thighs are motionless.

Sthairya : Firmness, Steadfastness, Steadiness.

Sthana : Standing posture, Location, Ignorance of voice registers, Occasions, Situations.

Sthanaka : The dancer stands in Sarna with her body kept straight and places her hands on the hips in Ardhacandra.

Sthapana : The dancer stands gracefully with an expressive face. The whole action is aimed at achieving Rekha.

Sthavira : Old dance.

Sthayi : Bhavadrstis, Glances in the dominant emotional fervours, Permanently dominant.

Sthayini : Permanent wife.

Sthira Movement : A glance fixed at a distant object.

Sthirahasta : The dancer stretches out the hands and lifts them, placing the feet together, and then after Lifting the hand above the shoulder, changes into the Pratyalidha Sthana. The hands. are separated.

Sthita : Steady, Slow.

Sthitavarta : One foot rubs against the ground and moves inwards. The other foot is moved away.

Sthula Gati : Stout person.

Stimita Movement : A fixed glance.

Subhadra : The metres with the second, fourth and the penultimate syllables long.

Sucana : Indication.

Suci : The hands are moved in harmony. One foot in Kuncita is raised and the knee is extended upward. Then it touches (the ground) with its forepart. She places one foot by the side of her thigh and then extends it forward pointing her toes.

Shanks : The dancer rests her left foot in Sarna, raises the heel of her right foot and touches the ground with the tip of the big toe.

Suci Viddha : Hands placed on the waist and chest respectively. The hands in Sucividdha are joined together. The dancer performs Suci with her left foot and turns round her hips.

Suci Mukha : The forefinger of the Khatakamukha. The hand is raised. The Sarpasirsa hands, with their thumbs touching the middle fingers, extend their finger tips obliquely.

Suddha : Unaffected, Pure, White.

Sukalasa : This is also known as Meni. Caris are used in this dance involving considerable movements of the feet.

Sukatunda : Beak of a parrot. The ring finger of the Arala hand is bent.

Sukatundavartana : One hand in Aviddha is moved near the chest with the palm turned down while the other hand is placed near the knee.

Sukumara : Delicate.

Sula : Trident.

Sunya : Vacant.

Sunya Movement : The pupils and eyelids are kept normally. The glance is vacant and does not see the object in front.

Sunyagara : Empty house.

Supta : Sleep.

Susira : Having holes, Hollow.

Susiratodya : Flute etc.

Suska Movement : A dim glance.

Suskaksaras : Meaningless letters.

Sutraka : Gold thread.

Sutras : Aphorisms, Principles .

Svabhavika Gati : Natural gait. Svajanavadha.

Svabhavika : Natural, Congenital. The nose is kept normally.

Svadhinabhartrka : One having the husband under control.

Svami : Master.

Svapna : Dream.

Svapnayita : Somnolent.

Svara : Accent. Notes.

Svarabheda : Change of voice and tone.

Svaramanthanrtya : The dancer is perform with the proper Hava, Bhava, Laya, Tala and Gati.

Svarasada : Feebleness in the voice.

Svarasadharana : Overlapping in notes.

Svarasadharanakrtas : Murder of Kingsmen.

Svarita : Circumflex.

Svastha Dasa : Relaxed state.

Svastika : Hands and feet respectively held together. The dancer performs Svastika with her feet. The dancer stands in Samhata with her feet in Kuncita. Then the feet cross in Svastika with their little toes touching each other. The dancer jumps with her hands and feet in Svastika. The hands are turned up and joined at the wrists on the left in Arala.

Svastikare Cita : The hands are moved successively in Recita and Aviddha. They are placed in Svastika and then they are separated and placed o n the hips.

Svastikaslesa : The Svastika hands are moved away from the shoulders.

Svastikavartana : The hands are moved in Vyavartana and crossed in Svastika.

Sveda : Sweat, Perspiration.

Syama : A dark face, Black, Green, Dark and Moody.

★★★★★

Tadana : Beating, To strike.

Taddhita : Nominal affixes.

Tala Instruments : Stringed ones.

Tala Samsphotita : Foot swiftly lifted up and placed forward, Hands show Talasamsphotita form palms together, left hand in Recita.

Talamukha : The hands should be changed from Caturasra to Hamsapaksa and they should be placed obliquely facing each other.

Talamukhavartana : The Talamukha hands are moved with Sausthava.

Talapuspaputa : Hand is held on the left side the foot is in the position Agratalasancara. One hand should be on the left side in Puspaputa.

Talarupaka : The dancer dances quickly to a very few talas. The dance is of various gaits.

Talasamchattita : Employ Dolapada cari.

Talasamsphotita : A leg is lifted quickly and put forward. The dancer moves in four directions. The feet are quickly thrown up in the Dandapada and the Atikranta Caris. The hands are clapped.

Talasanghattita : The hands are clapped repeatedly. Then the left hand, is moved in Recita. The feet rub against the ground in Agratalasancara. One side is in Vivartita. Then she places her right hand on her hips.

Talavilasita : Foot with toe and sole turned upwards, held high on the side, Palm of hands. One foot is raised and extended at the side with the toe and the sole turned up. The palms are bent.

Talodvrtta : The dancer quickly moves the forepart of her feet forward with the back of her toes touching the ground.

Tandava : Energetic.

Tani Movement : To look at a thing without knowing anything about it.

Tanta : A fatigued look.

Tanu Mandra : Low pitch.

Tapan : Pessimism.

Tapasvi or **Sadhu :** Blessed one.

Tapasvini : Ascetic ladies.

Tapta : The eyebrowss and eyelids are closed. The eyes are dull.

Tara : High pitch.

Tara Gati : High Pitch movement.

Tarala Movement : The pupils are moved.

Tarangita Movement : The eyes are gracefully moved like waves.

Tarjana : To threaten.

Tarksyapaksavilasita : The dancer performs Cakrabhraman, Hormayi, Dantu, Nihsanka consecutively.

Tarksyapaksavinodaka : The hands are moved together in Vartanasvastika at the sides.

Taruna : Matine, Excessive.

Taruna Movement : The eyes are distended at the corners and the rolling pupils denote desire.

Tata : Father. Stringed.

Tatpurusa : The Coordinating, Tauripa.

Taurika : Instrumenta list.

Tejas : Spiritedness.

Tharahara : The dancer shakes her body quckly and the arm are moved gracefully.

Tirascina Movements of Shanks : The shanks just touch the ground and move sideways.

Tirascinakugita : Nikuna is done by the foot first at its own side and then at the other side. Then it is placed in the middle and finally Nikutta is done obliquely.

Tiripa Bhramari : The dancer moves round her feet obliquely after crossing the feet in Svastika. The dancer moves to the left.

Tiryakarana : The dancer performs Bhramari in between some Karanas. The whole action is done repeatedly.

Tiryakjata Svastikagra : The hands are stretched at the sides and then they form a Svastika facing each other.

Tiryakkarana : The dancer jumps obliquely with foot and upon coming down, stands on the other foot.

Tiryakkuncita : The dancer bends one foot and repeatedly throws it down obliquely.

Tiryak Svastika : The dancer crosses her feet in Svastika and jumps obliquely.

Tiryak Tandava : One hand is raised first and then obliquely placed on the navel while the other hand is moved obliquely to the side.

Tiryatimukha : The dancer slides her feet quickly to the left and the sides.

Todana : Inciting. To push. Tolana.

Tolarupa : The dancer dances quickly in various talas with various Sankirna Gatis. This is also known as Kuvada.

Toranacalaka : The hands are crossed in Svastika and then they are separated. They are kept at the sides and again crossed in Svastika. They are placed on the head and separated.

Totaka : Quarrel.

Trasa : Fright.

Trasta : Frightened.

Trasta Movement : The eyelids are raised in fear and the pupils tremble. The eyes are wide open in panic.

Tratita Movements of Shanks : The heels remaining on the ground, to beat the ground with the toes.

Tribhangi Movement : To look at things through "the middle, the root and forepart of the eyes.

Tribhangivarnasaraka : The hands are rotated obliquely forward and at the sides. This may be done with both hands at the same time or alternately.

Trigata : Conversation of the trio.

Trika : Sacrum, Joint talk of a set of three persons, Units of three syllables, Triads.

Trikali : The distinctive characteristics of this dance are Gati and Gari. The head is moved in the following five way-Vidhuta, Akampita Dhuta, Parivahita and Kampita.

Trikona Cari : One foot rests on the toes. Then Nikutta is done in front, at the side and at the back. Finally the toes with the foot back in its original position.

Trikona Svastika : The hands are crossed in Svastika and then raised upto the left shoulder in Kuncita.

Tripatakavartana : The Tripataka hands are moved to the right and to the left. The wrists are also moved.

Trisamkhyata : Tripled in number.

Trisara : Three stringed necklace

Tritiyanrtya : The dancer dances in a fast tempo in the Trtiyatala. Lasyangas and Kalasa are performed with appropriate hand gestures.

Tryasra : The neck is slanted sideways. Triangular in shape Tryasra and Caturasra. Triangular.

Tryasra Movement : Tribhangi is done with an oblique glance.

Tryasra Movements of Shanks : The dancer rests her feet in Sarna with the heels inward and the big toes stretched out.

Tulya Tarka : Difference from similarity.

Tura : Musical accessories.

Turangini : The dancer moves round quickly touching the ground with the sides of her feet and stops in the middle of the stage.

Turlla : The dancer performs the Aslista Gati and Gajalila is quickly done. She moves her hands in the Padmakosa Vartana and performs Sthanas on all sides.

Tyaga : Readiness to sacrifice.

★★★★★

Ucca : High pitch.

Ucita Bhramari : To turn round the body obliquely after standing in Sarna.

Udaharana : Example, Parallelism, Exaggeration.

Udancita Movement : The eyes are open at the corners.

Udarata : Depth, Nobility, Exaltedness.

Udatta : Stately. Acute.

Udbhavana : Display.

Udbheda : Disclosure.

Uddhata : Haughty, Vehemently energetic.

Uddhura Movement : To look at a certain thing with a desire to know everything about it.

Udghanita : The elbows are moved to the right side of the body with the hands facing each other. The feet are moved to the left side.

Udghatita Movements of Shanks : The dancer stands on her toes and touches the ground with her heels.

Udghatta : Feet in the Udghattita movement. Hands in Talasamghattita and then placed on both sides. The hands are clapped and one side is bent. The hands are moved in Udvesita and Apaviddha and the feet in Nikugaka. This is to be repeated with the left limbs as well.

Udghatyaka : Accidental Interpretation.

Udvahi : Mouth turned upwards.

Udvahita Movement : To raise both the side of the hips slowly. Lifted up, Raised, The chest is raised.

Udvahita Movements of Shanks : The shanks are raised.

Udvapi : The mouth is turn ed up to show a woman's pride.

Udvartana Movement : Circular and swinging movement. To run away the pupils.

Udvega : Annoyance, Distress.

Udvegi : Disgusted.

Udvejana : Expressing disgust.

Udvestana : The dancer performs Vestana at the back and stretches her feet in front.

Udvestita : The arms move out from the wrist in Vartana movement.

Udvestita Karana : The fingers, beginning from the force finger, are moved outward.

Udvrtta : The foot of the Aviddha (Cari) surrounds the other. Then the dancer jumps up and after moving round, places it on the ground. The action is repeated by the other foot. The hands in Hamsapaksa are waved like palm leaf fans. The hands, the feet and the whole body is stretched out in Aksipta.

Udvrtta Movement : The eyelids are raised and the eyes are open. The pupils move inwards.

Udvrttaka : Stretches the hands downwards on either side and performs with them the Viksipta Karanas. Suci is performed with the hands. The back is revolved. The dancer performs Lata and Katichinna at the end.

Udvrtti : To raise.

Ugrata : Ferocity, Cruelty.

Uha : Reasoning positive.

Ullasa : A rhythmic dance expressing. Bhavas.

Ullasi Movement : A glance expressing desire.

Ullekhya : Tattoo Marks.

Ullokita : To look upwards.

Ullola : The dancer waves her feet one by one in the air. The eyes are raised.

Ullunthana : Irony.

Ulvana : The Alapallava hands are raised,and moved.

Unmada : Madness, Insanity.

Unmatta : The feet are in Ancita and the hands move in Recita.

Unmattagati : Toe mad man.

Unmesa : Opening, To separate the eyelids.

Unnata : Lifted up, The chest is thrown out to represent a proud man. The face is turned up, The neck is raised.

Unnata Movement : To raise the hips.

Unnata Movement of Knee : The knees are raised to the height of the breasts.

Upacara : Service. Ways of attention.

Upadesa : Instruction, Advice.

Upadhana : The fingers of the Pataka hand are separated.

Upadista : Utterance, Pointed utterance.

Upagukcana : Surprise.

Upahasita : Laughter of ridicule.

Upakorana : Dramatic production.

Upaksepa : Suggestion.

Upama : Simile.

Upanga : Ancillary limb.

Upanga Abhinaya : Gestures of the minor limbs.

Upanyasa : Reference.

Upara : The whole body is moved round in rhythm.

Upasarga : Prefixes prepositions.

Upasrta : One foot is thrown out and the hands are moved in the same manner. The body is bent forward. The left hand and the left foot are let down. The right hand is bent. The Aksipta Cari is performed with the left foot. The hands are moved in Vyavrtta and Parivartita and placed in Arala on the right side of the body which is bent.

Upasrtaka : Employ Akshipta Cari and harmonize the hands.

Upasthayakas : Servant, Buddhistic disciple

Upavahana : Upohana.

Upavanas : Derivative secondary.

Upeksa : Indifference.

Upohana : Humming or producing low sound as preliminary to a regular song.

Urabhrasambadha : The Svastika hands are quickly separated, moved out and away and then turned towards each other.

Urahparsvardha Mandala : The Alapallava and the Arala hands are moved by turns on the chest and on the sides.

Uras : Chest gestures.

Urddhvastha : The arm is raised above the head.

Urdhvajanu : A Kuncita foot is thrown up, knee stretched on a level with the breast, hands in harmony with the dance. The other foot is kept motionless. The same action is repeated by the other foot. The feet are bent, the left foot being placed forward. The hands move in Vyavrtta and Avartita. The feet are in Kuncitapada and the knees are raised.

Urdhva Mandala : The hands are raised and moved in circles.

Urdhvavartana : The hands are moved upward.

Ureveni : The dancer crosses her thighs and rubs the ground with the sides of her feet.

Uro Mandala : The feet are moved out of Svastika and they perform Apaviddha. The dancer performs the Baddha and Sthitavarta Caris with her hands in Uromandala. The hands are move near the chest, one in Udvetita and the other in Apavestita. Two feet drawn away from Svastika position.

Uru : Thighs.

Urudvrtta : One hand is moved round and then arched over to the back of the thigh. The shanks are bent and raised. The heel or foot is raised outwards. One shank is a little bent while the other is raised.

Urupas : The Urupa is performed with Yati, Tala, Laya, Sthana, Cari and hand gestures.

Uruslita : The thighs and the feet touch each other. One side is a little bent and the left arm is raised.

Urutadita : The dancer strikes the ground with one thigh and the foot.

Uruvrtta : The thighs move in Vivartita. The feet move in Recita. One hand is in Lalita and the other is in Lata.

Utkampa Movement : The eyebrows, eyelashes and pupils are moved.

Utkanthita Movement : The reddened eyes are full of tears at the corners.

Utkarsana : Drawing up words.

Utkata : The dancer stands in Sarnanakha with her feet either in Sarna or in Kuncita.

Utksepa : Lifting up. The dancer throws up one foot which is bent, forward and backward upto the knee. To raise the eyebrows together or one after the other.

Utksipta : Raised. The face is raised. To raise the toes repeatedly.

Utksiptapatita : Raising and falling.

Utkuncita : The dancer throws up her Kuncita feet and places them forward one by one.

Utpala Mala : Kuvalaya Mala.

Utphulla Movement : The eyes are open with the eyelashes separated .

Utpluta Bhramari : The dancer stands in Sama. Then she jumps and revolves her body.

Utsaha : Enthusiasm.

Utspandita : The feet are slowly moved inwards and outwards in Recaka.

Uttama : Superior.

Uttamavanade : Proceeding towards excellent park, temple etc.

Uttanvancita : The shoulders and the elbows are bent. The hands in Tripataka are moved obliquely.

Uttaratantra : The supplementary treatise.

Uttdna : Palm kept up ward.

Utthapaka : Challenge.

Uvartita Movement : The eye brows are raised.

★★★★★

Vacika : Verbal utterance, Pertaining to the words.

Vadha : Killing.

Vadi : Sonant.

Vadya : Instrumental. Drums.

Vaghiti : Nervousness.

Vaiaradya : Proficiency.

Vaikyavidhana : Popular modes of address.

Vaimanasya : Depression.

Vainava : Originating from Vina or lute.

Vaipota : The dancer moves her head in Vidhuta and Kampita and all the four Recakas.

Vaisakha : The feet are placed obliquely three talas and a half apart. They are turned sideways. The thighs are motionless. Vardhamana is performed with the feet.

Vaisakharecita : Hands, feet, hips and neck to be Recita, the hip and the neck also and the whole body in vaisakhasthana.

Vaisika : Gallant.

Vaisikopacara : Services of the Gallant.

Vaisnava : One foot is in Sarna and the other after being slightly bent is extended to the front obliquely. The feet are placed two talas and a half apart. One of them is raised while the other is placed obliquely with the toes pointing sideways. The shank is slightly bent. Sausthava is observed.

Vaivarnya : Change of colour, Lack of lustre.

Vajra : Thunderbolt.

Vakkeli : Repartee music, Musical instrument.

Vakra : Curved. The eyes are moved up and down at the corners.

Vaksah Svastika : The feet cross each other in Svastika. The hands move round in Recita near the chest which is arched. The heels are joined together.

Vakya : Words.

Vakyabhinaya : Verbal representation.

Valambita : Second the fourth and the last two syllables are long

Valana : To move the pupils obliquely. Turning.

Valana Movement : To turn the thighs, to do which, the knees must be turned inwards.

Valavyajanacalana : The fore arms are raised to the shoulders alternately. Then they describe a circle near the ground.

Valaya : Bangles.

Valgitas : Vaunting.

Valita : Hands to be Apaviddha, feet to be in Suci Cari. Trika turned round (lower part of the spine) Moved. One hand is thrown out while the feet are in Suci. The hips are turned round. The body is slightly twisted round while the foot of that side, towards which the body is moved, touches the ground with the little toe. The other foot touches the ground with the big toe. The Lata hands are crossed at the elbows. The neck is turned sideways.

Valita Movement : To draw away the eyes and then to look back obliquely and repeatedly.

Valitavartana : The Khatakamukha hands are joined at their tips with their elbows bent and raised.

Valitoru : Hands in Vyavartita and Sarivartita form and thighs as Valita

Valita Valitoru : The Sukatunda hands are moved in Vyavrtta and Parivartita simultaneously.

Vallis : Creepers bearing bulky fruits like gourds.

Valyas : Hairs.

Vama : Antagonistic.

Vama Bandha : Suci and Dandapada are performed by the right foot while Aparkranta and Suci are performed by the left foot.

The hips are turned round and the right foot moves in Parsvakranta. Aksipta and Dandapada are done simultaneously by the left and the right foot. The right foot performs Urudvrtta and the left foot performs Suci.

Vamadaksatirascina : The hands in Svastika are obliquely moved at the right and the left sides.

Vamsa : Flute.

Vanantas : Forest region.

Varadabhaya : The right hand points upwards with the palms facing outwards held at the side, while the left hand points downwards with the palms facing outwards and it is held at the same level as the hips.

Vardhamana : The feet are placed obliquely with the heels touching each other. The hands are placed in opposite directions in Hamapaksa.

Varitita : Hands bent at the wrist and place these hands on the thighs.

Varna : Caste, Colour, Syllable.

Varnas : Manner of utterance, Accents, Letters.

Varnasamhara : Meeting of castes.

Varsabhakridita : Alata is performed first. The hands move in Recita and then they are bent and inverted.

Varsas Gaura : Rose colour.

Vartanabharana : One hand is taken near the ear while the other is rotated. Then they are moved in Udvestita.

Vartanasvastika : One hand is separated from the other, is moved sideways with lightening speed and joined with the other. This is done repeatedly.

Vartita : Hands moved in Vyavrtta and Parivartita, the dancer bends them at the wrists. Then she places them on the thighs.

Vasakasajjika : Readily dressed up for Union.

Vasanta : Spring.

Varas : Eunuchs.

Vaskarana : Mnemonic patterns.

Vastu : Theme, The plot of the play.

Vastuetthapana : Raising the theme.

Vata : Wind.

Vatsa : Dear one.

Vatyavartia : The dancer performs Cakrabhrai man, Hormayi, Nihsanka and Dantu consecutively.

Vayas : Age.

Vayasya : Comrade.

Vega : Impetuosity, Agitation.

Vegini : The dancer moves quickly with the forepart or the heel of one foot. The hands assume Alapadma and Tripataka.

Velita : The neck with the face turned sideway.

Venuiguccaha : Braid of hair.

Vepathu : Trembling, Tremor.

Vepathuvyanjaka : The hands are moved alternately near the navel.

Vestana : The dancer encircles one of her feet with the other. This is also known as Valana.

Vestima : Wrapped objects.

Vestina : Vestima Encircling.

Vesya : Courtesan.

Vetika : Bangle shaped ring.

Vetra Asana : Cane seat.

Vi yoga : Separation.

Vibhakta : Proper proportion.

Vibhakti : Case endings.

Vibhavas : Detenninants.

Vibhinnapatra : Diverse characters.

Vibhrama : The metre in which the ninth, twelfth, the thirteenth and the last are long.

Vibhranta : Confused and excited.

Vibhranta Movement : The pupils are mobile and the glance is restless. The eyes are wide open.

Vibhrasta : The Corrupted ones.

Vibhtama : Confusion.

Vibodha : Awakening.

Vicara : Deliberation.

Vicaravastha : Reflective mood.

Viccheda : Separation.

Vicchitti : Disability.

Vicestitas : Activities.

Vicitra : The right foot performs Janita first and then moves in Nikutta. The left foot is moved in Aspandita while Parsvakranta is performed by the right foot. Then left foot performs Bhujangatrasita, Alata, Suci and Apakranta successively while in the same manner the right foot performs Atikranta, udvrtta, Parsvakranta and Viksepasuccessively and the right foot performs Apakranta. Finally, Bahyabhramaraka and Viksepa are preformed. Variegated. Smartly trimmed.

Vicitralohadi : The dancer stands sidewise to the audience and moves her body obliquely like a wheel .

Vicyava : The feet are separated from Samapada and they pound the ground with their toes.

Viddha : The corners of the eyes and the pupils are cast down. The dancer crosses her feet in Svastika and then swings one of them to the front and assumes Kuncita with the other.

Vidhana : Conflict of feelings, Scheme of falling.

Vidhi : Rules.

Vidhita : Refusal.

Vidhrta Bhramari : The dancer moves her whole body and looks down.

Vidhuta : Spreading of the mouth obliquely. The head is moved obliquely in all directions.

Vidrava : Running about excitedly, Panicky commotion. Excitements.

Vidusaka : Jester.

Vidyudbhranta : The dancer throws up one of her feet in front and moves it round quickly over her forehead in all directions. Then she places it on the ground.

Vidyudvilasita : The dancer performs Cakrabhramari, Dantu Nihsanka and Hormayi consecutively.

Vidyut : Lightning.

Varana : Warding off obstacles.

Vighnas : Malignants spirits.

Vighnavintiyakas : Malevolent.

Vighurnita : Rolling.

Vigraha : War.

Vihasita : Open laughter.

Vihasita Movement : The eyes are open and they do not wink.

Vihastatva : Bewilderment.

Vihrta : Mild. The right foot performs Janita and Nikuttaka and the left foot performs Aspandita. Then the right foot performs Udvrtta, Suci and Aksipta successively while the left foot performs Alata and Parsvakranta. The hips are turned round. Dandapada is performed. Suci is performed by the left foot and the hips are again turned round. Finally the right foot performs Bhujangatrasita while the left foot performs Atikranta. Want of response.

Vihvala Movement : The pupils are agitated.

Vijnata : Fully comprehended.

Vikaras : Upsetting tendencies.

Vikarsana : Dragging. To remove.

Vikasi Movement : A wide glance to look at things carefully.

Vikatthana : Boasting one.

Vikosa : Full bloom.

Vikosa Movement : The eyelids are wide open and the eyes do not wink. The pupils are restless.

Vikosita : Full blown.

Vikrsta : Expanded, Rectangular, The nostrils are dialated. To look vacantly at the sky.

Vikrsta Movement : The eyes are cast down sideways at the corners.

Vikrta : Pure and Modified.

Vikrta Rava : Terrific noise.

Vikrtalankara : Misplaced ornaments.

Vikrtavesa : Unseemly dress.

Vikrusta : Crying loud in the form of full throated sing.

Viksepa : The dancer extends one foot in front and bends it repeatedly. Throwing up, To throw.

Viksipta : The hands and the feet are thrown backward and in the same manner they are moved sideways.

Viksiptaksiptaka : The hands and the feet are thrown up and down.

Vikunita Movement : The eyes are contracted and only a part can be seen.

Vikunita : The nostrils are contracted.

Vilambi : Slow. Delayed.

Vilambita Laya : Slow temps.

Vilapa : Lamentation.

Vilasa : Amorous gesture, Graceful Bearing.

Vilobhana : Allurement.

Vilokita : Looking round, To look bacwards.

Vilolita : Apakranta is performed and the right leg crosses the left in Svastika. The hands are joined at the wrists.

Vilulita Movement : A distressed look.

Vimalajala : The third and the last ones are long.

Vimarsa : Deliberation, Pause. Vimarsa. Sandhi.

Vinata Movement : A straight, wide and cast down glance.

Vinaya : Humility.

Vinigfihana : The lower lip is drawn in.

Vinigirina : The eyes are open and they are full of tears.

Viniguhana : Concealing.

Viniskranta : The eyes want to leave their sockets.

Vinita : Disciplined cultured.

Vinivartana : It is Motita performed turning backwards.

Vinivrta : The face is turrned aside. Suci Viddha is performed first. The hips are turned round and the hands are moved in Recita.

Viparyaya : Inversion.

Vipluta : Distressingly disturbed.

Vipluta Movement : The eyelids tremble and then become motionless.

Viprakirna : The Vastika hands are separated.

Viprakirnavartana : The hands are moved in Udvestita and separated. The left is then placed on the left side, the right on the right.

Vipralabdha : Jilted by the lover Pause and deliberation.

Vipralabha : Deceived.

Vipralambha : Love in Separation.

Vipriya : Disgust.

Vira Movement : The eyes are fully open, excited steady. Heroic, The dancer comes forward from a distance with her left hand in Sikhara and the right hand in Pataka.

Virahotkanthita : Distressed due to separation.

Virakta : Hostiles.

Virama : Cessation, Stop.

Virodhana : Altercation.

Virudibandhana : One hand forms a triangle and describes circles in front and at the sides.

Virupa : Not fitting, Unnatural.

Visada : Despair, Agony.

Visadini : Sorrowfully dejected.

Visama : Unevenness, Metrical defect.

Visamasancara : The left foot is encircled by the right and the right foot is encircled by the left.

Visama Suci : The Suci feet are stretched apart simultaneously, one forward and the other backward. The knees and the ankles of these legs must touch the ground.

Visamsthula Movement : To look through the eyebeows.

Visandh : Hiatus.

Visanna Movement : The eyes are wide in dejection and they wink.

Visara : Expansion.

Visarga : Giving away, Closure , Spreading out, The lower lip is opened away from the upper. To send forth.

Visarjana : Dismissal.

Viskambha : One hand, placed in Suci, strikes the other while one foot is in Nikuttaka. Then the left hand is placed on the chest. The right foot assurnes Suci while the right hand assumes Alapadma. The left hand returns to the previous pose.

Viskamhhapasrta : Pataka hands should be performed with the hands in Recita.

Vislista : The dancer stands in the Parrsnividdha, Sthana and separates the feet.

Vislista Movement : To look at nothing due to anger.

Vislistavartita : The hands are crossed in Savastika and one hand is obliquely lowered. Then they are moved up and down at the sides.

Vismaya : Astonishment.

Vismita Movement : The eyelids are wide open and the eyes are still and raised.

Visnukranta : One foot is put forward and bent as if to start walking.

Vistara : Consists of four kinds of strokes.

Vistara Dhatus : Many other things.

Vistaraja : Growing out of amplitude.

Vistari Movement : The eyes are open.

Visuddhakarana : Pure Laughter.

Visvara : Absence of proper notes.

Vita : Lecher, Parasitic hangeron.

Vita Gati : Lecherous one.

Vitalita : Flapped, To strike the eyelids accidentally.

Vitarka : Deliberation.

Vitarkita : Guessing, Signifying conjectural guess.

Vitarkita Movement : The eyelids are raised, the pupils are fully open and they move downwards.

Vitata : Spread up.

Vivadi : Pisonant.

Vivarita : To raise the eyelids.

Vivartana : Contraction of the lower lip. Rolling, Narrowing, Turning, To turn the pupils aside.

Vivartana Movement : To turnround by drawing the heels inward. It is also described as Nivartana.

Vivartananrtya : The dancer dances to the Dhruvatala moving her left or right side of the body.

Vivartita Movement : The hip is turned round. The pupils are rolled upwards.

Vivartitaka : Hands and feet thrown out and turned round, hands to be Recita. The hips are turned round.

Vivrta : The lips are kept apart.

Vivrta Movement of Knee : The knees are stretched out.

Vivrtas : Open

Vivrtta : The hands and the feet are thrown out. The hands are moved in Recita.

Vivrtta Movement : To move the hips.

Viyoga : To separate.

Viyukta : Separated.

Vrida : Bashfulness.

Vridita : Ashamed.

Vrksa Bandha : Four talas are done as in Padmabandha. The first half of these are done first and the last portions are done together. The hands and the feet are gradually moved forward. The rest is done to a different tala.

Vrsabhakridita : Employ Alatacari both hands in Recita gradually taken to Kuncita and Ancita.

Vrsabhasana : The knees are placed on the ground together or separated. This is done with Sausthava.

Vrscika : The hands are bent over the shoulders and one foot is bent and turned towards the back. The dancer bends her body far back.

Vrscikakuttita : Assume the Vrscika Karana and make the Nikuttita movement of the hands. One foot is moved in Vrscika

Hands which are to be moved over the shoulder in Nikutta.

Vrscikapasrta : The Vrscika karana accompanies the Lata hand. Bend the hands, in the same position, to touch the tip of the nose. The hands change into the Udvestita Hastakarana. The Ailgahara is finished by doing Nitamba, Karihasta and Katicchinna.

Vrscikarecita : One foot moves in Vrscika while the hands cross each other in Svtika. Then they are moved in Recita and Viprakirna.

Vrtta : Metres.

Vrttantasya : Non-omission of essential features Anupaksaya in the play.

Vrttas : Parivartas .

Vrttas Viramas : Caesura etc.

Vrttis : Graceful styles, To Roll, Prose, Passage, Dramatic Style, Simple movement.

Vsesana : Distinction.

Vtddhas Sthaviras : Old dames.

Vyabhicari Bhavas : Transitory states.

Vyabhughna : Slightly.

Vyadhi : Illness, Sickness.

Vydhiprabhavam : Resulting from ailment.

Vyahara : Declaration.

Vyajima : Indicating objects.

Vyakarsana : Drawing out, To pull.

Vyaksepi Movement : To look backwards through the corners of the eyes.

Vyakta Mukta : Clearly liberated, Fully open.

Vyalapankti : Snake group.

Vyalika : Mixed feeling.

Vyamsita : Then they move up and down in Viprakirna.

Vyanga Darsa : Displaying deformed limbs.

Vyanjana : Indication.

Vartaka : The hands are quickly moved out to the sides and the elbows point at each other. Then they are joined while being turned to the ground.

Vyasanabhighata : Adversity or sudden attack of people.

Vyasangi Movement : The eyes look at a distant object.

Vyavartita Karana : The fingers, beginning from the little-fingers are moved inward.

Vyavastiya : Assertion.

Vyayama : Exercise.

★★★★★

Yajnakriya : Sacrificial rite.

Yajnavit : Expert on Yajnas.

Yamaka : Alliteration.

Yamas : Watches.

Yana : To lead.

Yantras : Machinery.

Yathasthita : Literal. Ordinary.

Yati : Caesure, Pause. The dancer dances Laga with various beautiful rhythmic movements and gaits.

Yauvanabheda : Stages in the growth in adult-hood.

Yuks : Even ones.

Yukti : Decision.

Yuvati Strigati : Young women.

★★★★★

Zenana : Inner apartment.

★★★★★